The
TRUTH
ABOUT
TRUANCY

BEN WHITNEY

KOGAN
PAGE

London • Philadelphia

First published in 1994

Apart from any fair dealing for the purposes of research or private study, or criticism or review, as permitted under the Copyright, Designs and Patents Act, 1988, this publication may only be reproduced, stored or transmitted, in any form or by any means, with the prior permission in writing of the publishers, or in the case of reprographic reproduction in accordance with the terms of licences issued by the Copyright Licensing Agency. Enquiries concerning reproduction outside those terms should be sent to the publishers at the undermentioned address:

Kogan Page Limited
120 Pentonville Road
London N1 9JN

British Library Cataloguing in Publication Data

A CIP record for this book is available from the British Library

ISBN 0 7494 1416 2

Typeset by DP Photosetting, Aylesbury, Bucks
Printed and bound in Great Britain by
Biddles Ltd, Guildford and King's Lynn.

Contents

Dedication

This book is dedicated to those young people who feel they have no place in our education system...

> Teachers telling me to take my earrings out, and reminding me of what the uniform was. I stopped going because I was sick of being belittled. I couldn't see how what you wore affected how much you learnt. I wanted to be independent; I had a mind of my own. I was now a young adult and I felt I should be able to have a say and that my views should be respected. (School-leavers Project, Islington LEA)

... and to all those parents, teachers and professionals doing their best to convince them otherwise!

Acknowledgements

My thanks are due to all those from whom I have learned a great deal about education social work in the last few years: children, families, teachers and my colleagues in Staffordshire Education Welfare Service and elsewhere. I am particularly grateful for the support and encouragement I have received through the National Association of Social Workers in Education, including Arnold Dry, who died suddenly while this book was in preparation. The opinions expressed are, however, entirely my own responsibility. They do not necessarily reflect the policy of Staffordshire LEA or its Education Welfare Service.

Ben Whitney
Summer 1994

Introduction

A CONFUSED PICTURE

As with most of its social problems, Britain is confused about truancy. We do not know whether to be tough or tender and exactly who to blame. In fact, the overwhelming majority of children go to school regularly – probably as high a percentage as those adults in employment who should be at work on any given day. Yet the government seems to hold a view of armies of deviant teenagers starting down the slippery slope towards a life of crime – a perspective which doesn't always seem to fit with reality and which has never been proven to be true.

Experts

Experts, as always perhaps, don't agree on what we are talking about. What is a 'truant' and how many of them are there? How are they different from a 'school refuser', a 'school phobic' or a 'child with emotional and behavioural problems'? Indeed, does the word 'truancy' really describe the phenomenon? Can you truant for six months at a time? Are you a truant if your mum keeps you at home to look after the baby while she goes to work or if your reason for keeping away is fear of failure or personal worries?

Should school attendance be compulsory at all? Confusingly, there are those on both the left and the right of the political spectrum who suggest that compulsion in education makes little sense and that there would be no problem if we simply took a different view. Some argue that schools oppress children and that staying away is only common sense; others say that if children and parents don't want to use the opportunity there should be no obligation on the state to provide it.

Parents

Parents, normally welcomed and courted as key partners in the education process, find themselves in this context being lectured, blamed and even criminalized for their failure to act responsibly. Parents don't actually *have* to send their children to a school and some choose other perfectly legal ways of ensuring that they are 'properly educated'. Why then make attendance a matter of enforcement? Surely it's more a question of entitlement – making sure that appropriate opportunity is available to parents to enable them meet their children's needs?

For so many parents, burdened by poverty, poor housing, family breakdown, redundancy and all the rest, yet more moral exhortations delivered by those for whom such issues are simply statistics, mean nothing. If their own education was a disaster, and we are constantly being told how bad it was in previous decades, how can they be expected to see the point of it today? Yet don't parents have some obligation towards both their own children and society at large, no matter what needs they may have of their own?

Schools and LEAs

Headteachers and governors now find the quality of their school being judged by its raw level of 'unauthorized absence' rather than by how well they are trying to deal with it. They are being encouraged by the DfE to persist with the problem child rather than exclude them too readily, at the same time as being given greater freedom to keep such children out in the first place by restricting at least some of their entry. Pastoral staff are under constant threat as an ever-increasing emphasis is placed on performance and success in measurable examination performance, yet many teachers feel they are being asked to do much more 'social work' with less and less recognition of what they need to do it.

LEAs are being urged to 'crack down' on truancy and give it higher priority, though many have cut their welfare provision in the face of requirements to delegate more of the available resources direct to schools. Every possible pressure is being placed on schools to distance themselves from LEAs and their influence, yet the statutory duty to act on attendance still lies with the LEA alone. How can LEAs fulfil this responsibility towards children in schools over which they have little or no control?

The law

The law about absence from school is less clear than most people assume and its effectiveness in changing behaviour is unproven. The regulations about how to keep the figures are constantly changing and markers of registers are beginning to wonder if they are really private detectives in disguise, so complicated has the system become! League-tables are legally required, but their content is a matter for considerable discretion. For all the claims made in the White Paper preceding it, the Education Act 1993 added nothing new to the available powers, and much of the legal framework for responding to absence is contradictory.

The Children Act 1989 gave LEAs a new resource – education supervision orders – but few have responded with much enthusiasm and the DfE rarely mentions them, preferring instead a generally more punitive tone. Care proceedings can no longer be used to deal with the poor attender; indeed the whole social work climate for children in difficulty has been moved by the Department of Health away from intrusive intervention to supportive voluntary services. There is a division at the heart of the government about what laws we need and how we should use them.

Education welfare officers/social workers

EWOs/ESWs do not know whether we are supposed to be friends or enemies of the young people and parents with whom we work. We are the key professionals, but are rarely heard in the debate. Are our clients 'mad, bad or sad' and does anything we do actually make much difference anyway? Where is the profession going now that LEAs are diminishing in significance? Who are the 'customers' of our services in the new education market: schools, parents, children, politicians, society? We are constantly being told how important we are in combating truancy, with over 100 years of experience behind us, but many are feeling uncertain about what the future may hold.

Children

Which brings us, at last, to the pupils. Here, as usual, they seem to come at the very end of any catalogue of those who have an interest in education. Recent research has at least sought to give them a voice, to ask *them* why they stay off school, but there is little evidence that anyone is taking much notice of what they say. None of the reforms of recent years has given children any more right to be consulted or involved in decisions about their own education.

Staying away is still one of the few choices they can make for themselves.

More change to the curriculum could mean a more attractive, flexible package which may win the support of those who feel out of place, but there are few real alternatives for most children. They are as confused as the rest of us. Treated as young adults one moment, expected to conform without question the next. Even when they are old enough to marry or have children of their own they can still be sent home for having their hair too long (or too short!). What's the point of school if all there is at the end is unemployment?

THE AIMS OF THIS BOOK

So why risk adding to the muddle by writing another book, and under such a grand-sounding title at that? My only defence is that I don't believe the vast majority of educational professionals are content simply to stagger on as we are. This book reflects the perspective of education social workers. We accept that truancy is a 'bad' thing. It always has been. Bad for schools, bad for families and society and, primarily, bad for the children and young people involved who find themselves as a result even more disadvantaged in our competitive society than they might otherwise be. We want things to be better for them. If you lack any sense of idealism, read no further.

But, for all our good intentions, we simply don't know what to do about those children and parents who do not share our vision. No one seems to know what to do, even if some are quick to make simplistic judgements and propose ill-considered solutions. Increasingly, with all the emphasis on figures and fines, schools are being tempted to push the reality of truancy under the carpet: to marginalize those who choose not to participate; to manipulate the statistics in order to make it look as if there is no problem; to stereotype, blame, condemn and criticize those who do not fit in; to put it all down to the increasing moral indolence of other people. It's so much easier than trying to find the truth. I hope this book will at least lead you closer to that alternative.

My purpose is essentially practical: to help teachers and others to address issues of non-attendance, but with a word of caution first. There is no point in launching into frenzied activity without being clear what we are talking about and what we are trying to achieve. Chapters 1, 2 and 3 are intended to ground the issues in their proper context, both historical and contemporary, theoretical and legal. The rest of the book aims to outline good practice; for schools in Chapter 4 and at the inter-agency level in Chapter 5. In Chapter 6, however, I return to more philosophical issues and in particular to the assertion that we do not currently have all the answers we need. Too much emphasis on 'doing something' may obscure these wider and, in my judgement, unavoidable questions for the future.

1

'Always with us'

CHARITY, COMPULSION AND COMPETITION

A natural reticence?

Truancy, like poverty, has a lengthy past history, and the two have always been closely related. Such is the suspicion of the British, education has perhaps never received universal approval among the population as a whole, despite the best intentions of the legislators. The Prime Minister himself said in a television interview at the beginning of 1994 that as a nation we do not take kindly to being told what to do by politicians (though it appears that not all his Ministers agree with him!). It must be wise not to imagine that we are the first generation ever to consider how we overcome this natural reticence when it comes to school attendance. Whether things are any worse now than at any other time in the past is not at all clear.

The history of educational provision in England and Wales is marked by a series of landmark pieces of legislation. Acts in 1870 (Forster), 1902 (Balfour), 1944 (Butler) and 1988 (Baker) form the major milestones, with many more local signposts in between. Whether the 1993 (Patten) Act, the longest of them all, will come to rank alongside these only time will tell. That is certainly its intention. Significantly in the current context of concern about truancy it restates the basic legal requirement on parents to ensure that their children attend at a school where they are registered pupils, the first such restatement for 50 years (see Chapter 2).

Beginnings

The story begins, of course, well before 1870, with an education system based on class and charity. Much of the early evidence recognizes the difficulty in seeking to establish a national and universal system of educational provision, not least because of the question of whether people actually wanted such a thing. First, however, there was the need to establish that not everyone who did want it had access to it already. The Parliamentary Committees on the Education of the Lower Orders in the Metropolis and Beyond between 1816 and 1818 brought to the country's attention that:

> A very large number of poor children are wholly without the means of Instruction, although their parents appear to be generally very desirous of obtaining that advantage for them.... The greatest advantages would result to this Country from Parliament taking proper measures, in concurrence with the prevailing disposition in the Community, for supplying the deficiency of the means of Instruction which exists at present, and for extending this blessing to the Poor of all descriptions. (Maclure, 1965, pp.18–19)

Whether the poor themselves saw this as such a major disadvantage might not always have received so positive an answer. I doubt they were often asked! From the beginning, education has been as much about the needs of society as a whole as for the benefit of the individuals concerned. It is no different today. Indeed, this probably provided one of the primary motives for those who were anxious that the 'lower orders' should receive an education appropriate to their needs and station rather than be susceptible to the more revolutionary ideas then more in vogue on the mainland of Europe.

However, the sense of education as a right, and therefore demanded by the poor as part of their entitlement to a basic quality of life, should not be underestimated, even if there may have been a hidden agenda in the minds of many of those concerned about their plight. Neither should the very genuine sense of charitable concern and philanthropy be dismissed out of hand, though at this time the distinction between religious and secular education is very hard to draw.

Education must have been as much about increasing the moral and religious stability of the cities and remote rural areas as it was about equipping the poor with the skills they needed to serve them better in their domestic life or employment prospects. But although there were plenty of signs of inter-denominational rivalry as each group sought to use education to increase their influence over the masses, there is also evidence of cooperation at the local level, at least on the more secular aspects of the curriculum.

Too poor for school

With the Sunday Schools for 'ragged' children had come the recognition that some were too poor to present themselves at even the meanest school, and that attempts to encourage them might not always be welcomed. The evidence of Rev William Gurney, Rector of St Clement Danes to the Select Committee of 1816 was that:

> There are a great many mendicants in our parish, owing to the extreme lowness of some parts of the neighbourhood, and the more children they have, the more success they meet with in begging, and they keep them in that way; so that in the weekday we could not get them to a day-school without some different measures were adopted; neither are they fit to appear in some of them as they are; and on Sunday they get more by begging than they do on any other day of the week, because more people are out and about; we tried the experiment in several instances, by giving clothes to the most ragged, in order to bring them decent to school; they appeared for one Sunday or two, and then disappeared, and the clothes disappeared also. (ibid, p.23)

Many families, school pastoral staff and education welfare officers would no doubt still recognize the same difficulties, trying to stretch minute school clothing grants across those families in receipt of Income Support and therefore entitled to a free school meal. How much greater though is the contrast with those children and young people for whom clothing is no longer simply functional but a badge of identity and credibility among their peers. How much more desperate it must feel in the 1990s not to be able to compete without resort to charity. (It is still in such a context that any call for compulsory school uniform must be judged against its likely effect on attendance.)

First signs of reluctance

In the early 19th century, concern about absence related as much to absence from church as absence from school and the debate raged about whether educational opportunity should be dependent on attendance at the Established Church on Sundays. In his evidence to the 1834 Report on the State of Education, Rev William Johnson, Clerical Superintendent of the National Society, demonstrates a remarkable capacity to handle concepts of 'authorized' and 'unauthorized' absence which a class tutor of today might do well to copy:

> As regards our own school, we are certainly most anxious to

have the children with us on the Sunday, but there are continually some absent on that day; reasons are assigned for their
absence, and those reasons admitted; but I should not think
myself justified, according to the understood principle and
practice on which the directing committee of the Society act, to
allow children to go to a dissenting place of worship. (ibid, p.29)

Mr W F Lloyd, Secretary to the Sunday School Union, however,
indicated just how great the problem was perceived to be of
ensuring that some children attend at all:

A very important part of the population we cannot touch at all; I
refer to the most degraded of the poor; I mean the children of
trampers and beggards and gipsies, and people of that kind.
Sometimes, by extraordinary efforts, we get some of these
children into the school, but they are off again almost immediately; and those are the children from whom a very large
proportion of our prisons are peopled. Now the difficulty is,
how to get these children under instruction, and how to keep
them under instruction. (ibid, p.32)

Still today we recognize that children from travelling families are
less likely to be able to attend school than others, by the provision of
special support teachers and welfare staff and even by a legal
recognition that children prevented from full attendance by virtue of
an itinerant lifestyle only have to achieve 200 attendances a year
rather than the full school year for everyone else of almost 400
sessions (Education Act 1993 s.199(6)). The link between poor
attendance at school and future criminality is a matter for some
debate, but that many in our prisons have missed out on education,
for a variety of reasons, could scarcely be denied. The relationship
between the two, however, may be more complicated than a simple
case of cause and effect.

The Newcastle Report
The Newcastle Report of 1861 was the most comprehensive review
so far of the state of 'Popular Education in England'. Commissioners
visited local areas in each specimen type of community: agricultural,
manufacturing, mining, maritime and metropolitan and visits were
also made to several countries elsewhere in Europe for comparison.
All but about 100,000 of the estimated two million children of the
poor were in schools of some kind, at least up until the age of 11,
though many of them were of dubious quality. Most children spent
four to six years attending a school, but only 5 per cent continued

beyond the age of 13. (By comparison, only 320,000 children were reckoned not to belong to the 'poorer classes' – a sign that the middle classes, a major outcome of extended educational opportunity, had not yet emerged.) (ibid, p.71)

There was clearly no overall consensus about the validity of extended universal education. In his evidence to the Newcastle Report, Rev James Fraser, who later became Bishop of Manchester, said:

> Even if it were possible, I doubt whether it would be desirable with a view to the interests of the peasant boy, to keep him at school till he was 14 or 15 years of age. But it is not possible. We must make up our minds to see the last of him, so far as the school day is concerned, at 10 or 11. We must frame our system of education upon this hypothesis; and I venture to maintain that it is quite possible to teach a child soundly and thoroughly, in a way that he shall not forget it, all that is necessary for him to possess in the shape of intellectual attainment, by the time that he is 10 years old. (ibid, p.75)

Matthew Arnold, one of the Newcastle Commissioners, raised even more philosophical questions and began to ask about the meaning of 'compulsory' education and people's commitment to it. Perhaps, he argued, in a report of 1867, there is something about the British way of life which leads us to value education less than other things. Such a culture must be taken into account in any attempt to enforce education on those who may see other priorities as more important:

> The difficult thing would not be to pass a law making education compulsory; the difficult thing would be to work such a law after we had got it. In Prussia, which is so often quoted, education is not flourishing because it is compulsory, it is compulsory because it is flourishing. Because people there really prize instruction and culture, and prefer them to other things, therefore they have no difficulty in imposing on themselves the rule to get instruction and culture. In this country people prefer ... politics, station, business, money-making, pleasure and many other things; and till we cease to prefer these things a law ... cannot be relied upon to hold its ground and to work effectively. (ibid, p.82)

Are things necessarily so different now? Many of those struggling to motivate children and their families to have a positive view of education in the 1990s would affirm much the same sentiments. The whole society and its priorities are involved. It is not simply a matter of individual behaviour, but an age-old battle to help some young people and their parents to believe that education is of much value and that it is a worthwhile investment of their time and energy, against the powerful background of a social context which may be saying the complete opposite.

Many families simply do not accept the basic premise that education matters; their experience tells them otherwise; unemployed parents, siblings and peers are all around them, some well-qualified and even over-educated for the available opportunities. To 'politics, station' and the like must be added leisure, relationships, sport, 'Skive TV', computer games and so many other things which interest them more and which send conflicting signals about the long-term value of school. Now, as then, passing a law and persistent nagging will not be enough. Can the law actually change the way people think, feel and behave? We shall come back to these profound questions later.

1870–1944

Forster, introducing the 1870 Education Act, had no such worries. Too many children were being badly taught or not taught at all. With the establishment of local School Boards came a duty to frame bye-laws to ensure the education of all children between the ages of 5 and 12 (later in this chapter I indicate how they went about this task). Penalties could be levied upon parents for failing to make proper arrangements, thought they were restricted to five shillings, unless reasonable excuse could be given. Interestingly, the defences in the 1870 Act are virtually identical to those defined by the 1993 Act: sickness, unavoidable cause, no school within a reasonable distance and education being provided in some other way. Education was compulsory, though attendance at a school might not be – a distinction still valid, though often overlooked.

By the Balfour Act of 1902, concern was more about the education of older children and the first signs begin to emerge of the inexorable lengthening of the educational experience and therefore of its period of compulsion. With the recent advent of County and Borough Councils, it seemed appropriate to pass the responsibility on to them as part of a general and more integrated approach to local services. Local Education Authorities were born and, in his speech outlining the Bill, Balfour looked forward in a way which can only bring a smile to their successors in the 1990s:

> No practical man will tell me across the floor of this House that he expects Parliament or the country will ever deprive the

municipalities of powers they have so admirably used. I would therefore say to the advocates of School Boards that ... if he wants a universal authority – one which can really coordinate education – it can only be to the municipalities that he can turn his gaze. (ibid, p.152)

Such sentiments held sway until the late 1980s; it is impossible to say whether they will ever be true again. The 1918 Act saw the raising of the school-leaving age to 14, with an expectation that it would soon be 15, and it enabled LEAs to develop their support services more extensively; a vital recognition that not all that is needed for a proper education system takes place within schools. Concern began to be expressed about the poor health of many children and that they could not learn effectively. School medical services were founded as part of a growing back-up strategy. The idea of 'continuation studies' was born, in which older children would continue their education on a part-time basis beyond the minimum leaving age. Little provision was actually made however, due to the increasing economic recession.

The curriculum
By the 1930s questions were again being asked about the curriculum and its relevance. Attendance is one thing; actual useful learning is another. The Report of the Consultative Committee on Primary Education of 1931 has an amazingly contemporary ring. Sir Ron Dearing would surely recognize the following:

No good can come from teaching children things that have no immediate value for them ... to put the point in a more concrete way, we must recognise the uselessness and the danger of seeking to inculcate ... inert ideas – that is, ideas which at the time when they are imparted have no bearing upon a child's natural activities of body or mind and do nothing to illuminate or guide his experience.... While there is plenty of teaching which is good in the abstract, there is too little which helps children directly to strengthen and enlarge their instinctive hold on the conditions of life by enriching, illuminating and giving point to their growing experience. (ibid, pp.191–2)

The Spens Report of 1938 was the first to recognize that universal education up to the age of 16 was becoming appropriate, if not immediately achievable, in order to offer all children equal opportunity for learning. Few seem to have questioned whether the commitment of young people and their parents to extending the period of compulsion would be easily obtained, though as early as the Norwood Report of 1943 there was talk of the importance of 'child-centred' education in order to make the provision relevant to their needs.

1944–1988

The 1944 Butler Act, probably the key landmark of them all, established the system of primary, secondary and tertiary education in which each child would be educated in the appropriate school 'according to his age, ability and aptitude', though the technical schools never really established themselves and the inherent elitism of the grammar school inevitably made those 'selected' for secondary moderns feel as if they had failed. The Act also recognized for the first time the importance of nursery education, though again provision lagged behind.

By creating a Minister for Education, the Act represents something of a centralization of responsibility in contrast to the period after the 1902 Act, but LEAs retained their local role of enforcement of attendance. Parents were still not required to have their children educated at a school where it was being done 'otherwise' but School Attendance Orders were introduced for those situations where the LEA took the view that the child should be admitted to a school. Once registered, parents could again be prosecuted for failure to ensure their children's regular attendance.

During later years there were considerable changes to the structure of educational provision, but the attendance requirements remained unchanged. There was, however, continued concern about 'truancy' and undoubtedly one aim of the move towards comprehensive mixed-ability schools was to remove the stigma sometimes associated with the secondary modern which led to low morale, poor motivation and high rates of absence.

But still, in 1974 for example, the Schools Sub-Committee of Staffordshire LEA noted the growing concern of secondary schools about levels of truancy and called for an expansion of the Welfare Service in response. If there was a 'golden age' of school attendance, it was longer ago than this, presumably during the 1950s and 60s when many established conventions were being questioned as inappropriate for a modern society and a progressive welfare state was in full swing. Much effort was made, however, in response to the final raising of the school-leaving age to 16, to try and encourage greater commitment from older pupils, especially through alternative, non-examined curricula.

The 1980s saw a period of unprecedented change in educational structure culminating in the 1988 (Baker) Act and all which flowed from it, in particular, the first ever National Curriculum. As well as such further moves towards centralization there was also a wide range of reforms intended to give greater financial and decision-making control to school governing bodies and parents, including the choice to become directly funded by Whitehall rather than through the LEA. LEAs were opened up to a more market-oriented philosophy in which many services had to be sold to schools on a more competitive basis, though education welfare/social work services, at least in theory, remained relatively intact. There was, however, a growing sense of accountability to schools as the 'customers' of the service (see Chapter 5), and some LEAs have moved to a system of partial delegation of the budget as a consequence.

Beyond 1988

The 'Parent's Charter' first issued in 1991 and reissued in 1994, is one of a whole series of such documents, and represents a typical 1990s way of doing things. It is about both rights and responsibilities, about encouraging parents to take more control over their children's education, while at the same time reminding them that they, in turn, are subject to the control of central government and political decisions about resources. Parents are partners one moment and treated with suspicion the next; most are reckoned 'good enough' to deserve proper recognition and involvement, but some are seen as failing to give their children a good example. Despite the provisions of the Children Act 1989, many parents separated from their children still found schools unwelcoming. Even in the Charter, the DfE made no effort to recognise their needs. Parental involvement is still highly dependent on how much opportunity is offered.

But the climate is radically different and schools do have to be much more accommodating to parents than previous generations of headteachers would ever have thought possible (or desirable). Schools have become much more 'parent friendly'. Many, however, still see school as a place to keep away from; a focus of authority figures and judgement about their particular lifestyle. The parents in these families show all the reluctance of their 19th century forebears to pick up their new powers and use them.

Raising standards
Most of the reforms of the late 1980s and early 1990s were said to be about raising standards. In order to do this, competition

between schools has replaced the previous model of coordinated provision across a given area or community. Parents are advised to shop around rather than accept the LEA's choice of school for their children. Schools will come and go in the future: they must attract parents and pupils to survive; if they succeed they will attract more; if not, they will close. New schools may grow up in their place.

Within this context, levels of absence have become a means not only of judging parents, but also of judging schools. Among numerous league-tables of performance which governing bodies must publish, 'truancy rates' have a key place. This emphasis on the school as in large measure responsible for the attendance of its pupils represents a major shift, several implications of which will be explored in later chapters.

Yet the LEA remains, so far, responsible for the legal enforcement of attendance, as well as for a range of other duties towards children with special needs or in difficulty. Education can never be addressed in isolation. Some within the government have been calling for a return to more traditional methods and 'old-style truancy officers' as part of a campaign to recover 'basic values'. Yet a key characteristic of the British education system has always been a recognition that 'education' can never be entirely separated from 'welfare'. Some may regret this but it is an inescapable fact over generations. It is to the story of these provisions, in LEAs and beyond, that we must now turn in order to complete the picture.

WAGGING, BOBBING AND BUNKING OFF

The School Attendance Officer

In 1865 the Council of the Reformatory and Refuge Union took nine attempts to find a proper man to become their Attendance Officer. Eventually they appointed Mr William King whose duties were:

- to seek out neglected children in the streets;
- to search out the person whose duty it was to care for them and who had failed in that duty;
- to restore outcasts to their parents or guardians and to introduce them to the Ragged School or Industrial School, or in the case of offenders to reformatories;
- to visit each Ragged School within a certain district and other like institutions so as to confer with the masters and matrons to secure their co-operation;

- to provide, if necessary, immediate shelter and food while enquiries were being made;
- to enter in his journal full particulars of his work, visits and enquiries;
- to receive and carry out in each case the directions of the Committee;
- in order to perform these duties satisfactorily, attention will be restricted only to as many cases at once as can be investigated thoroughly, so that cases may be satisfactorily concluded, rather than engage superficially in a number. (NASWE, 1992)

Difficulties in recruitment, the problem of unmanageable caseloads, potential conflict of expectations between your employers and your schools – all these would be recognized by Mr King's successors in the 1990s – along with the lack of mention of any pay for his services! It was the Act of 1870 which created the term 'School Attendance Officer' and which empowered local School Boards to appoint officers to enforce their consequent bye-laws and the requirements of the Industrial Schools Act of 1866.

The 1876 Education Act sharpened parents' duties more clearly but already rather more than mere enforcement of attendance at school was seen to be involved in the Officer's duties:

1. To see that the name of every child between the ages of five and fourteen years (unless previously exempted from attendance at school according to law) was on the register of some public elementary school, or to satisfy himself that a child was under efficient instruction in some other manner;
2. To secure the regular and punctual attendance at school of children whose names were on the school roll;
3. To make enquiries and report with regard to,
    (a) the remission of school fees in necessitous cases,
    (b) applications for part-time labour certificates. (Quoted in Stevenson and Hague, 1954, p.1)

The Officer had to identify children in his area, investigate reasons for their absence, authorize other provision, approve working arrangements and, crucially, assess for help with the cost of education for those unable to afford it. In many ways the work must have been more complicated then than today as there were other, quite legitimate, tasks in which children could be engaged and considerable judgement and discretion must have been required.

To these duties were added others within the next 30 years: the Employment of Children Act 1903 introduced greater control of working hours and street trading and, a milestone if ever there was one, the Education (Provision of Meals) Act 1906 required an assessment of those children unable to benefit from education through lack of proper nourishment.

A developing role

Already then, the 'welfare' tradition was strongly established, seeking reasons for problems and trying to resolve them rather than simply carrying out regulations. Up until the passing of the Children Act 1948 a wide range of duties was required, summarized by Davison (in Stevenson and Hague, 1954, p.2) as follows:

> In addition to visitation for absentees, such duties as: arranging transport to schools, bringing to official notice, for the information of the school medical officer, all children in need of special educational treatment, so that the most suitable arrangements may be made for their education, rescuing children and young persons found to be in need of care or protection or in moral danger; reporting on the home surroundings of children and young persons appearing in the Juvenile Courts, making inquiries on behalf of the Ministry of Labour in respect of young persons between fourteen and eighteen years of age who are not in employment and enforcing their attendance at Unemployment Instruction Centres; and many other duties which he is, from time to time, required to perform.

As for the public perception of these responsibilities:

> One of the marked results of the way in which officials have discharged these extended duties is that the resentment of former days, which was frequently exhibited by some parents towards the School Attendance Officer, has gradually given place to a spirit of appreciation and friendliness on the part of both the parent and the child. He is now regarded by the majority of people as the parent's advisor and the children's friend. Prosecution now forms a very insignificant part of his duties.
>
> The Attendance Officer has developed into a social worker. He comes into contact with the homes and parents of children as probably no other municipal officer does with the possible exception of the Health Visitor, and combines with his various duties a considerable amount of welfare work. (ibid, p.3)

The 1940s and beyond

All this before the 1944 Act – so we would have to go back a long way to find the powerful and forceful figure imagined by the traditionalists. Even allowing for the fact that many of the 'social work' functions might properly be seen as having passed to the children's departments and their successors in social services departments, few within the profession would seek a return to a method of gaining the public's confidence already discredited by the turn of the century!

Law enforcement does form a part of the work, as it does for any social worker whose primary interest is children's welfare, but not for its own sake alone. The prosecution of parents may form a limited part of creating a climate that school attendance is important, but there is little or no evidence that it produces what society really wants: a population which believes in education and its value in their lives. This seems to be true even for those individuals who actually go through the prosecution process. Very early on Mr King and his colleagues discovered that you have to win people over, not frighten them into submission.

However, statutory responsibilities must not be overlooked. The 1944 Education Act enabled LEAs to bring children before the Juvenile Court instead of, or as well as, taking action against their parents. Such a child was deemed to be 'in need of care and protection' and the Juvenile Court was empowered to place the child in the care of the local authority. This power was confirmed by the Children Act 1948 and the Children and Young Person's Act 1969.

It can rightly be argued that with this legislation the responsibility for children's welfare gradually moved away from the Attendance/Welfare Officer and on to the officers of the children's committee of the local authority. This is a trend which has continued ever since, culminating in the Children Act 1989 which finally ended the power of the LEA to have children placed into care for failing to attend school. Under the 1969 Act, non-attendance at school was one of the clear grounds for such intervention, though it became increasingly discredited and ineffective to the point where it is scarcely to be missed.

The Ralphs Report

Meanwhile, the education welfare profession was going through difficult times: still left with significant responsibilities under education, employment and other law but increasingly being left behind by professional developments and greater training opportunities amongst their local authority social work colleagues. Only a handful of social services departments incorporated education social workers into their structure under the Seebohm reorganization of the early 1970s, largely on the grounds that insufficient resources were available to ensure that their educational emphasis could be maintained.

In addition, there were some advantages in retaining a welfare perspective within the education context in order to ensure that children's whole needs were addressed, especially for those children identified as having 'special educational needs' from 1981. To have removed all of the 'social work' influence into an entirely separate department would not, in my opinion, have ensured that the welfare needs of children at school were adequately safeguarded, especially in the current climate of so much pressure on local school budgets.

The Ralphs Report of 1973, a report of the Local Government Training Board, is still regarded by education welfare officers with some affection in that it drew attention to the nature of their work as indistinguishable from social work but that it was being undertaken with markedly less opportunity for training, promotion and reward. It recognized that children's emotional and social problems were becoming ever more complicated and that EWOs/ESWs still represented the front-line service for many families in trying to deal with them.

New skills were required, a fact made even more relevant by the emerging significance of child protection services, a factor only just being recognized in the early 1970s. Staff were constantly being lost to social services departments (SSDs) and there was a danger that officers of the necessary calibre would not be available in the future in sufficient numbers to maintain the required services.

The present day

On the whole this hasn't happened, although terms and conditions of employment within the education welfare service remain way below those of their colleagues both in schools and in other local authority social work departments. Despite this, there have been determined efforts to raise the skill level of staff (about 20 per cent of whom now possess formal social work qualifications), but also recognizing that there is a specific task of education social work which retains much of the best of the past.

Many would even argue that there is more actual 'social work' going on in many education welfare departments (though not all) than in some SSDs, now subject to the pressures of the purchaser/provider split which has radically changed the role of the field social worker away from direct work with families. In terms of actually spending time with clients, trying to help them solve their problems (perhaps, admittedly, a rather old-fashioned definition of social work) I doubt this assertion could be refuted.

Many other skills are required: EWOs/ESWs usually have to assess their own referrals without the protection of a case-management system; they have to work continuously in inter-agency structures, often having to balance various conflicting demands and expectations; they still have enormous workloads, sometimes having to prioritize their time over five or even six high schools (and all their feeder primaries), with little or no administrative or clerical back-up. And they still have to handle the delicate balance between befriending and enforcement as their predecessors have done for generations. In the debate about truancy, and in the care of society for its children's welfare, they surely still have something important to say?

REFERENCES

Maclure, J S (ed.) (1965) *Educational Documents, England and Wales 1816–1963*, London: Chapman and Hall (out of print).

National Association of Social Workers in Education (1992) Source unknown. Circulated by NASWE.

Stevenson, J and Hague, L (1954) *Handbook of Child Care Law*, (4th edn), London: Pitman (out of print).

2

The Law on School Attendance

EDUCATION ACTS 1944/1993

A new priority?

The White Paper *Choice and Diversity – A New Framework for Schools* (DfE/WO, 1992), which preceded the Education Act 1993, made much of the importance of school attendance. After all the changes of the 1980s it was as if the government had just discovered that there was not much point in reforming the school curriculum if children were not there to receive it. Under the heading 'Going to School, Staying There and Learning', section 1 says:

> There is too much truancy from our schools. This undermines our educational system. It means that some schools are turning a blind eye, and some parents are not fulfilling their side of the bargain by meeting their legal obligation to see that their child attends school. Worst of all, it can lead to much unhappiness amongst school children themselves, as well as to greater problems for the community.
>
> This Government sets great store by ensuring that children go to school and stay there throughout the school day. We are no longer prepared to allow schools to turn a blind eye, and have therefore placed them under new legal requirements.... All maintained schools will have to publish their truancy records which will be a powerful incentive for all the under-performing schools to do better. (pp.5–6)

The White Paper placed a clearer emphasis than ever before on the school as responsible for its own levels of attendance. This is a considerable change from previous thinking and reflects, quite rightly, the sense that with greater autonomy must come an acceptance of greater responsibility. As LEAs have been distanced from the day-to-day running of schools, so governors and headteachers must now be seen to be tackling their own problems. Hence the need for published figures relating to levels of absence so that schools can be as accountable here as in other areas of measurable performance.

However, LEAs retain the statutory role for ensuring attendance, not least because they can take a wider perspective than school staff and are able to facilitate a variety of responses where needed. Neither parents nor schools are on their own in tackling non-attendance and they are entitled to feel that a range of support services is available to help them in their shared task. The law then provides a structured framework, as set out later in the White Paper, if resolution cannot be found in other ways. This extract suggests that there is an answer to every eventuality; many would doubt whether this is true:

> ... there will be cases where the school at which the pupil is registered fails to secure regular attendance, as well as cases where children are not registered at any school – including children whose parents wish to educate them at home. The LEA will continue to be best placed to liaise with social services departments over some of the causes of persistent truancy, and to make educational judgements about alternatives to school education. LEAs will therefore continue to have the duty to enforce school attendance by serving School Attendance Orders, seeking Education Supervision Orders, and taking cases to court where necessary. (ibid, pp.28–9)

Duties and offences

Children do not break the law if they stay away from school. There is no offence of 'truancy' and no criminal proceedings can be taken against any child, no matter how bad their attendance. Since the very beginning, the powers of enforcement have been only against parents. Children are not legally responsible for getting themselves educated; it is difficult to see how they could be. Recent legislation, despite some claims to the contrary, has not changed this situation.

Criminalizing children for not going to school has been suggested again recently. It would be unlikely to achieve a great deal not least because, as we shall see in the next chapter, it would be extremely difficult to know which absences would constitute an offence. How will the anxious, depressed or abused child be distinguished from the rest? How many absences would be enough for the law to be *ance*

...it would we do with the children when convicted?
...iot truancy leads to crime, or is in some way associated
...not in itself a criminal activity on the part of the child.
...damental to understanding what is going on and how to
...it.

Und...r s.36 of the Education Act 1944, parents have a basic duty to ensure that their child receives 'efficient full-time education' according to their 'age, ability and aptitude and any special educational needs he may have' while of compulsory school age, either 'at school or otherwise'. This normally extends to the leaving date in Year 11, not just to the 16th birthday, which may be several months earlier. (Only those children not registered at a school for at least the previous year reach the leaving age on their 16th birthday.)

The vast majority of problems will be resolved voluntarily. But the 1993 Act gives LEAs a duty to deal with two possible situations where parents have failed to act appropriately and where court

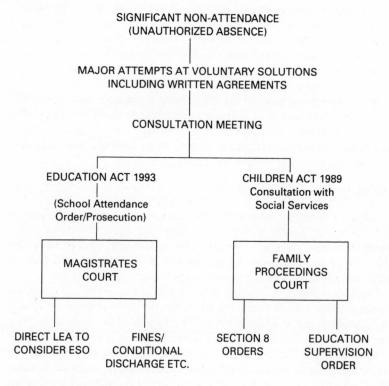

Figure 2.1 *LEA powers*

action can be used if judged appropriate (see Figure 2.1). So unless there are further changes in the law, there will always need to be at least some provision at LEA level for every child in the country. It is hard to imagine headteachers wanting to take over this legal role themselves, though the possibility of it being dealt with in some other way cannot be ruled out for the future.

School attendance orders (Education Act 1993 s.192)

This section enables the LEA to serve a notice requiring a parent to register their child at a school of their choosing, once it has been established that they are not being properly educated 'otherwise'. No response to this notice within a given time will result in the service of the order itself, naming a school chosen by the LEA. This might happen in a number of circumstances:

- the LEA has inspected the arrangements for home education made by the parent and decided that they do not constitute sufficient provision;
- parents have moved house and failed to register their child at a new school within a reasonable period;
- travelling families have not made alternative provision and the children are not receiving any education;
- parents have not yet enrolled their child at a new school on secondary transfer, perhaps after failing to secure a place at the school they would prefer;
- families settling from overseas have not made any arrangements to educate their children since arriving in the country.

The offence (s.198) is failure to comply with the order, so no court proceedings are required unless the parent fails to act once it is served. Once served, an order lasts for the remainder of the child's school career. It is relatively uncommon to get this far in the process and there are very few actual prosecutions for non-compliance. However, the power can be useful in requiring parents to make a decision rather than letting a situation drag on unresolved.

Although some who have commented on the 1993 Act do not seem to have realized it, such orders are therefore only of any significance when it comes to children *not registered* at any school. They are not designed to deal with 'truancy' at all. They do not order a child to attend; they order parents to register them. Parents who are educating their child outside the school system are not automatically breaking the law, though to avoid these procedures they must inform the headteacher/LEA in writing of their decision and allow the provision they make to be inspected. (The education they provide does not have to cover the whole National Curriculum). Slightly more complicated arrangements apply if the child has special educational needs or if a grant maintained school is involved, but the principles are the same.

Prosecution of parents (Education Act 1993 s.199)

This section makes it an offence by the parent if their child fails to attend regularly at the school where they are a registered pupil. There is no definition of 'regularly' but technically the parent is guilty by the fact of any absence, *unless* certain defence grounds apply, as set out further in s.199. Even one absence to which these grounds do not apply could be considered an offence though, of course, prosecution requires persistence before it could be considered reasonable.

Lateness, *after* a reasonable period for registration, could be seen as an offence, though it is much more difficult to apply the law if the child registers and then leaves the building. Parents could almost certainly argue that they could not be held responsible for this failure if they had ensured that the child was there at registration. Indeed, like s.198, s.199 is not really designed to deal with 'truancy' either, but with irresponsible action by *parents*. It is again their neglect of duty which is the issue here, not misbehaviour by the child. Where parents have done everything reasonably possible but have failed to change the child's negative attitude to school, we are clearly talking about something other than the situation envisaged by this provision.

Grounds for defence
As was noted in Chapter 1, the defence grounds in the 1993 Act are substantially the same as those which have applied ever since the element of compulsion was first defined:

- absence 'with leave';
- sickness or other unavoidable cause;
- days of religious observance;
- failure by the LEA to provide transport where under a duty to do so;
- a travelling lifestyle (minimum 200 attendances).

The most significant change relative to the 1944 Act is the clearer prominence of 'leave' (given by a person authorized by the school to do so). If the child is absent with the approval of the school, whatever the reason given by the parent, *no offence is being committed*. This makes the decision by the school over whether or not to authorize an absence under the Education (Pupils' Attendance Records) Regulations 1991, absolutely crucial in determining whether or not the LEA has grounds for prosecution.

It is unfortunate that the 1993 Act itself makes no reference to authorized and unauthorized absence. It would have made things much simpler. This, after all, is the basis on which the evidence is being collected. But if all the absences have been explained satisfactorily, to the point where the school has authorized the child to be absent, this clearly means that 'leave' has been given.

It could even be argued that this extends to whether or not an officer of the LEA has the right to intrude into the family at all, though there is a legitimate role in gathering information about reasons for absence where they have not been obtained by other means. However this is primarily the responsibility of the school; *schools authorize absences, not parents or LEAs*. It is a judgement which headteachers must make after reasonable investigation. Here is a clear reinforcement of the sentiments in *Choice and Diversity* but much misunderstanding and confusion is caused unless everyone is consistent on this point.

It has been my frequent experience that meetings called to consider the possible prosecution of parents have first had to establish whether or not the school has collected any evidence. It may be quite difficult to do so. Parents may deliberately seek to mislead or even tell blatant lies. How far are staff expected to go in checking whether a child was actually ill? But if no question has been raised, and absences have all been authorized, it will be impossible for any LEA to take action. The parent has a cast-iron defence.

An element of discretion
There are a variety of grounds on which schools may exercise their power to grant leave. These are set out in various regulations and relate to situations such as, for example, family holidays during term-time. Regulation 12 of the Education (Schools and Further Education) Regulations 1981, gives the governing body, acting through the headteacher, power to grant up to *ten days* leave in any year to enable the child to participate in a family holiday. (The regulations do not actually say so but this is usually taken to mean a calendar year.)

This is not an automatic entitlement – headteachers may choose not to grant any such leave and some schools are now making this a condition of entry, though it is difficult to imagine the LEA taking any action if the child missed only a few days. But the discretion is limited to two weeks unless the circumstances are unusual. Such exceptional leave should be authorized by the governing body itself on a case-by-case basis. The defence grounds would not then apply to any disputed period (as long as it was left unauthorized), for example a second holiday in October when two weeks had already been taken in May.

This is often an issue for children from ethnic minority families who may leave the country for weeks or even months at a time to visit relatives. Treating such parents as committing an offence would not normally be reasonable. In these circumstances it may be best not to treat this as absence at all but to remove the child from the school roll for the time they are away and re-admit them on their return. This avoids large numbers of authorized absences (which now have to be declared), even where the governing body has given special consent. This can cause problems in an over-subscribed school, but if the headteacher chooses to mark all the absences as authorized, the LEA will be under no obligation to act in response.

Leave can also be given for other legitimate reasons such as family bereavement or to enable children to prepare for examinations, though the regulations do say that such power should be used sparingly. Where proper approval has been obtained from the LEA for the child to take part in an entertainment or when the child needs regular medical treatment during school time, leave can again be granted. *Each* authorized absence should be marked in the register with the appropriate code showing the grounds on which leave has been given for that session.

If there is uncertainty about the validity of the explanation provided, clarification must be sought *before* deciding whether or not to authorize it, or as soon as practically possible, using an interim mark in the meantime. As will be explored later, it is best if a school has a clear policy on such matters so that everyone – staff, parents and children – is fully aware of its implications for practice (see Chapter 4 for comments on good practice in marking registers in the light of DfE guidance).

The effectiveness of prosecution

Prosecution of parents is always a last resort and, by and large, the legal framework tends to be more useful in setting the boundaries than in resolving individual problems. It is helpful to have a law which sets out parents' duties to ensure that their child is educated, but this does not mean that taking court action against them is always the best way of proceeding where there are difficulties. Many parents do not know the law and respond better when it is pointed out to them. But those who are not persuaded by information and warnings may not be persuaded by action either, especially if they do not feel entirely in control of their teenager's behaviour. Rewarding a child for their rebellion by punishing their parent is not likely to help the family develop more appropriate structures of authority.

As a means of actually reducing absences or returning children to school, prosecution is unproven, though there are those who argue that it acts as a general deterrent to others and that this may be more important than its direct effect on those who go through it. When the new registration regulations were introduced in 1991, together with a call from the DfE for more prosecutions, it was also acknowledged in a written Commons reply that there was *no* published evidence supporting their effectiveness. Many people seem to assume that prosecution should happen, whether or not it works.

Such limited research as has been done, for example that reported by Solihull LEA in 1991, suggested that court action was of very limited value in changing people's behaviour. Many situations deteriorated even further after prosecution, some parents had to be prosecuted more than once and there was no evidence of any deterrent effect on others (Solihull LEA, 1991).

Procedures

For a magistrates court hearing, the headteacher is required to testify in writing that the attendance record produced is an exact copy of the register. The register is the evidence. This is why the issue of whether or not absences have been authorized is so crucial. There can be no question of the LEA glossing over any shortcomings in the register. For schools using computerized registration systems similar principles apply (though a computer print-out cannot, of itself, be produced as evidence). All evidence must meet the 'six-months rule'; that is, the period of attendance and absence covered must not go back any further than six months from the date when the LEA begins the proceedings.

Parents can be fined up to £1000 on conviction, though the vast majority of fines are far smaller and may be as little as £10 or £20. Alternatively, many parents are given conditional or even absolute discharges. Fines must still take into account people's ability to pay even though the much tighter 'unit fines' system no longer applies. Anyone who has care of a child may be prosecuted – you do not have to have 'parental responsibility' as defined by the Children Act 1989 – as well as people with parental responsibility who live apart from the child. School attendance is, however, usually seen as part of the duty of care on the person actually looking after the child day-to-day. Until October 1991 it was possible, though extremely rare, for a parent to be imprisoned for repeated offences, but this is no longer available, except for non-payment of fines.

Wider issues

Most LEA procedures drafted with the authority of the Education Act 1993 are designed to keep people out of court wherever possible; voluntary action is always to be preferred and must always be fully explored first. Where parents are patently failing to discharge their proper responsibilities, ie, not coming to meetings, refusing to cooperate or allow home visits, encouraging a child to work in school hours or moving on to avoid detection, and are thereby putting their child's educational opportunity at risk, prosecution has its place as a way of demonstrating the seriousness of the situation.

In my experience at least such situations are the exception and some parents in that position will even consider the fine a price worth paying (I was once offered a wodge of crisp tenners to drop the matter!). Victory in court can appear rather hollow if the child continues to be absent. If the source of the problem is a breakdown in family relationships, parental inexperience or stress, housing difficulties, poverty or children with emotional and behavioural problems, prosecution may well make the situation worse and lead to a significantly increased threat to the welfare of the child concerned.

At this point education law has to recognize that it does not have the field all to itself and that any decision to prosecute parents must always be the best course of action available once all other avenues have been considered and rejected. LEAs cannot operate in isolation and, ironically, this has become increasingly significant in recent years, just as the DfE seems to be expecting the opposite. As we have already seen in Chapter 1, the law about children and what is best for them takes us well beyond the confines of education alone. This has never been more true than it is now.

CHILDREN ACT 1989

A welfare framework

Although the Department for Education seems rather reluctant to admit it openly, the Education Acts are not the only framework within which authorities must act in response to a child's poor attendance at school. Other legislation defines how responses might be made when the focus of the issues is on the child and their needs rather than strictly on parental failure as above. Indeed, the Education Act 1993 places a duty on the LEA to consider this option *first*, before initiating any action against the parents. There has always been a 'twin track' approach which has placed as much emphasis on 'welfare' as on enforcement. (See Whitney, 1993, Ch.4)

School has long been seen as a critical area of a child's life in which problems within the family and community will inevitably be expressed. Many children in trouble or distress will demonstrate their difficulties either at school or by refusing to go. Any other expectation would be wholly unrealistic, as if the child could be one person from 9.00 till 3.30 and another when the school is closed. Problems may have nothing at all to do with school as such. As a result, education welfare officers/social workers occupy a unique position in helping school staff to be aware of these wider issues and setting education within a wider social context.

As with the excessive emphasis by some on outdated and outmoded methods of enforcement against parents by 'truancy officers', there is much ignorance and misunderstanding here too. One of my professional roles is to deliver training to school staff and governors on attendance and absence issues and how we can deal with them. I often use a 'brainstorming' exercise in which I ask the participants to list all the possible things which may happen to a child as a consequence of not going to school. What powers do LEAs and local authorities actually have when families run into difficulties? Many answers reveal that even those working most closely with children are 20 or even 30 years out of date in their thinking.

Some talk of children being 'sent away' or 'taken away' from their parents and put in 'approved schools' or 'borstals'. (Incidentally, many children still fear these consequences as well and it seems to do little or nothing to affect their behaviour.) Many assume that 'truancy' is an offence and that the child could be 'dealt with' in a Juvenile Court. When the new secure training orders were in the news, some said that children would now be sent to 'secure units' for not going to school. Even more would talk of children being 'put in a home' or, if they are teenage girls, of them being in 'moral danger'.

Some talk of 'secure' special schools which such children could be made to attend. Some clearly wish that corporal punishment could still be administered even though they do at least recognize that such a response would now be inconceivable. It comes as a surprise every time that *none* of these powers exists. They have all failed and been replaced by a quite different approach. Much of the frustration amongst headteachers and others about lack of action by LEAs is caused by expectations which simply cannot be met.

The Children Act in summary

When the Children Act was implemented in October 1991, it was hailed by the Department of Health as the most wide-ranging reform of the law about children this century. It created a wholly new framework for dealing with the welfare of children. The key themes which are relevant in this context can be summarized as follows:

- provision within the Act for dealing with poor school attendance requires the same approach as that which applies at every other point – the welfare of the child is the 'paramount' consideration;
- the parental relationship is more about responsibility than rights, now expressed in the central legal concept of 'parental responsibility';
- parents are entitled to help in caring for their children. The work of agencies should be seen as a service, with statutory powers being used as little as possible;
- parents should be helped to resolve problems on a voluntary basis, with courts only intervening as a last resort;
- parents should be treated as partners by agencies wherever possible – they are part of the answer rather than the cause of the problem;
- children have a right to be listened to and consulted when decisions are being made about their lives;
- agencies must work together, cooperating in providing a network of support for 'children in need'.

A new approach

The Children Act is not about giving local authorities increasing power to intervene in family life. If anything it is a movement in the opposite direction. While it is important to have safeguards in place which protect children from abuse and give necessary authority in situations of 'significant harm', the onus is on the agency to prove that it can do a better job than the parents. Courts cannot be asked to make orders unless it can be demonstrated that things will be better for the child with the intervention than they would be without it.

Care orders and court action for child protection have shown a significant fall as a result of the Act; increasingly it is expected that agencies will resolve problems voluntarily, with children remaining in their families unless it is absolutely necessary to remove them for their immediate protection. Where orders are granted, they are generally shorter than before and parents retain their legal relationship with the child throughout, even if it is necessary to curtail their involvement for a period. In terms of legislation, if not yet of attitude, the culture has moved away from the idea of punishment and separation in favour of a model of protection and support.

This philosophy does not sit too comfortably with the more punitive tone which sometimes comes from the Department for Education. Indeed the Act is something of an anachronism in this context, despite the protestations of the Department of Health that the whole government is committed to its approach. Little has been done nationally to help schools to become aware of the Act's provisions; there has been next to no public information to promote its implications for education.

Children in need

But the Children Act is the only legislation there is for tackling absence from school and related welfare issues where it is judged that the focus of the problem is the behaviour and needs of the child rather than failure to act responsibly by parents. Its provisions must now set the boundaries, and all agencies are committed by the Act to an approach based on 'welfare' – the central concept of the legislation. A particular focus is Part III about 'children in need'. Children who are having difficulty attending school, excluded children and those at risk of it, and children with special educational needs, including emotional and behavioural disorders, should all be included in this definition. The Act gives local authorities, including education authorities (s.27), a *duty* to cooperate in providing services to help such children and their families, though sadly this is the part of the Act which has most clearly not been properly resourced since its implementation. The range of services which families need is often not there in reality.

The idea that education welfare officers might return to a threatening and punitive style at the same time as their colleagues in social services are seeking to offer the same child and his or her parents help towards resolving their problems through partnership, consultation, services, etc. is a nonsense. Any suggestion of a coordinated approach, centring upon the best welfare interests of the child, would have been abandoned.

Force has failed. There has been a public outcry in recent years against social workers 'taking people's children away' without justification. Children who went into care because they weren't going to school didn't go to school afterwards either. It simply exposed vulnerable children to all kinds of other risks. 'Approved schools' never delivered an acceptable standard of education and disrupted children's relationships with their parents, with long-lasting consequences.

Such responses have been rejected as counter-productive and ineffective. Putting children into residential settings away from their parents only breaks up the family unit and leaves us with angry and lonely young people littering the streets of our cities. Involvement should be positive not negative; supportive not critical. It should be about building up and sustaining the family, not breaking it up because we know best what they should do. All this is fundamental to the Act's approach.

Education supervision orders (ESOs)

The Children Act established new kinds of courts to deal with both 'public' and 'private' law applications about children. These Family Proceedings Courts (FPCs) do not deal with children who commit offences; they are dealt with quite differently in what is now called the Youth Court. The sole concern of the FPC is to consider issues relating to children's welfare – care orders, supervision orders, child protection and issues arising from divorce and separation.

It is in this context that LEAs are given a new power which *replaces* their previous power to seek to have children taken into care where they are not being 'properly educated'. Instead of, or as well as, proceeding against parents in a magistrates court, the LEA may make an application under s.36 of the Children Act to have a child of compulsory school age placed under its supervision for a period of one year in the first instance. In effect, an ESO makes the LEA responsible for ensuring that the child is educated, though there is a duty to work closely with both parents and child and take their wishes into account.

S.202 of the Education Act 1993 requires LEAs to consider whether an ESO is appropriate *before* prosecuting parents for an offence. In addition, a magistrates court hearing an adult prosecution may direct the LEA to consider applying for an ESO instead or in addition. This replaces their previous power to have a case transferred into the old Juvenile Court for care proceedings. The LEA does not have to seek an ESO if it is satisfied that the child's welfare is being safeguarded in some other way or that the order is not in the child's best interests.

Only LEAs can apply for these orders and they can only be made on application, ie, at the LEA's initiative. Social services must be consulted but they do not necessarily have to agree. The only other orders which can be made in these proceedings are Section 8 Orders (the replacement for 'custody' and 'access') where other issues to do with residence, contact, etc. may need to be resolved.

ESOs require lengthy preparation including detailed application forms (with a £50 fee for each child), records of attendance, written reports (including a school report) and written statements of evidence of what has already been attempted. These must all be submitted in advance, together with a plan of action outlining what will happen if the order is made, including any proposed changes in educational provision. This is to enable the court to decide whether what is proposed is in the child's best interests – just not going to school is not sufficient reason in itself to make an order. ESOs can be extended on application by the LEA or can be discharged early on application by any of the parties. Both the LEA and the child should normally be represented by solicitors.

Essex CC v. B

Government guidance (Volume 7 of the Children Act series) and an important test case (Family Law Reports, 1993) have established a number of issues about education supervision orders.

- They are not intended to force children into school: the relationship between the Supervisor and the child should be built on encouragement, not threat.

ESOs are designed to give vulnerable children the protection of an order so that they may be 'properly educated'. The supervisor must 'advise, assist and befriend' the child and their parents and has power to issue 'directions' setting out what they must do, but it is a fundamental misunderstanding to see any order under the Children Act as a punishment. Children are not 'sentenced' to supervision and such language should be avoided. Orders cannot be 'breached' by the child's failure to cooperate, though referral must be made to the social services department if the order is failing so that they can consider whether other services or orders may be appropriate.

Parents *can* be prosecuted for persistent failure to follow the supervisor's directions but this will be rare as orders would not normally be sought if the parents were openly hostile to the idea in advance.

- A court should normally make an order when asked to do so on the grounds that it is always better for the child to be educated than not to be educated.

The proviso in s.1(5) of the Children Act that courts should not make an order unless they are satisfied that it will be better for the child than no order, has led some LEAs to steer clear of ESOs altogether on the grounds that they cannot hope to demonstrate in advance that this will necessarily be true. Even with the best assessment procedures it is not possible to *prove* that an order will improve the situation. The ruling establishes, however, that an ESO is not a magic guarantee, but an attempt to make use of the powers provided by the order which have not been available before.

Judge Douglas Brown made it clear that all the LEA was attempting to do was to ensure that the child was educated. *Provided they can put together a credible plan*, such an attempt must always be better for the child than simply leaving things to drift on without resolution. Even in the face of parental indifference and limited hope of success, it might still be appropriate for the LEA to try all the means at their disposal rather than do nothing where no progress is being made in other ways. Applications should not be refused solely on the grounds that they might not work.

This is very important and, in my opinion, many LEAs have failed to take the opportunity presented by the Act to use its provisions in this way. The principle of 'non-intervention' does not mean 'do nothing'. It means only that orders should not be sought unless they are needed and without genuine attempts to resolve things by agreement first. If these have failed, and if the structure of the order *may* add something to an unresolved situation for which no other interventions have proved appropriate, they should be tried, unless they are clearly not in the child's interests or the LEA has no constructive plan to offer.

- Applicants and magistrates must pay careful attention to the 'welfare checklist' in s.1(3) of the Act.

ESO applications are 'family proceedings' just like other uses of the Act and the same welfare principle applies. They should be seen in the same way as any application by the social services – they are no different just because the LEA has the responsibility at this point.

Decisions must have regard to the ascertainable wishes and feelings of the child (though the child does not have a veto, they do have the right to representation of their views, if necessary independently of their parents); the likely effects on the child of making the order must be considered; their physical, emotional and educational needs must be promoted and full consideration given to the particular background and circumstances of the child as an individual.

The LEA must be able to show that the child's welfare is their paramount concern and expertise in devising plans and pro- grammes to promote their best interests is required. None of this is compatible with a view of education welfare officers as seeking to threaten children into school attendance on pain of punitive sanc- tions if they do not do as they are told. Annoying though it some- times is for all of us, you cannot *make* a child act in their own best interests; even with an ESO you can only advise and support them. 'Directions' may help in setting boundaries but it is not a crime for the child to ignore them.

The use of ESOs

The DfE, as with the rest of the Act, has been largely silent on the use of ESOs since issuing its guidance in advance. They are rarely if ever mentioned in the context of new initiatives to combat truancy. My informal canvassing of colleagues in other LEAs suggests that few have had extra resources to implement them or used them with any great enthusiasm. This is a mistake, for both political and practical reasons. Powers which are not used may be taken away. The last thing EWOs/ESWs need at this time is to be distanced from the Children Act and from practitioners in other agencies. In my experience, ESOs do work – at least some of the time – provided they are carefully targeted and are not seen as a universal panacea for *all* children whose attendance is poor.

To date my LEA has obtained around 30 ESOs (out of a school population of almost 150,000). In about two-thirds of the cases, some improvement in attendance has been achieved, with a few of the children moving from no attendance at all to full-time in main- stream schools, while others were satisfactorily attending a variety of alternative units, etc. Of course we do not know whether this would have happened anyway, but this is at least limited evidence that some children and families welcome the structured intervention of the order and respond more constructively as a result of the court process. There is an urgent need for national research to produce a fuller picture.

ESOs work best when schools work closely with the LEA; they are most at risk of failure where there is little mutual understanding and cooperation. It is unfortunate that court procedures do not usually enable anyone from the school to attend the hearing. This should not mean that the school feels isolated from the proceedings and a good supervisor will be constantly seeking to work with school staff. Regular reviews of progress are essential and it is best if everyone agrees that no one will act unilaterally (eg, about a possible exclusion) without full consultation first.

The power to give 'directions' to a child has sometimes been useful in helping them to appreciate the need to listen carefully to the supervisor and at least try to do what they are being asked to do. Some parents have found the support helpful and have made greater efforts than before to work cooperatively and present a united front to the child. Of course this hasn't always worked and it is particularly frustrating for all concerned when a child continues to refuse school, even when every possible effort has been made to help them. But a more draconian power might not work either; experience suggests that it will not.

This is all rather low-key and unspectacular. We would always prefer to plan packages of action with children and their parents on a voluntary basis and will go to considerable lengths to do so. More flexibility and variety in educational provision at the local level would be more useful than any number of legal powers as a means of resolving problems. But if we are going nowhere an ESO may help to free the log-jam. It is still early days and ESOs should not be overrated – but they have their place, I am sure of that.

'Significant harm'

There are some poor attenders for whom an education supervision order is not appropriate. Some children will not respond to this kind of intervention and many teachers and others are increasingly despairing of a small group of children about whom we are effectively powerless to act through the courts. I am not sure that legislation currently gives us all we need, but it has to be accepted that removing such children from their parents has proved generally disastrous in the past. Now, for a child to be made the subject of a care order, the court must be satisfied that they are 'suffering, or at risk of significant harm' and that this harm is attributable either to their being beyond parental control or to a lack of reasonable care (s.31).

So it is not enough *just* for the child to be beyond the control of his or her parents by, for example, refusing to go to school. They must also be suffering, or at risk of 'significant harm' as a result, *and* a court must be satisfied that the making of an order will be better for them than no order. Perhaps their behaviour and attitude will be even worse if they are removed from their parents' care against their wishes. What provision does the local authority have which is likely to bring about a response different from that which has been tried already? Unlike the previous Children and Young Person's Act 1969, no specific circumstances such as 'moral danger' or absence from school are defined as grounds for intervening. These are no longer factors which necessarily make care proceedings appropriate.

While missing out on education might cause the child considerable disadvantage, it is not likely, in itself, to be judged 'significant harm' and no social services department would seek a care order now on such grounds alone. Poor school attendance might be part of a wider package of concern where, for example, the parent is deliberately putting the child's welfare at risk or failing to protect them adequately. But if the child is rebelling over school, but is well cared-for in every other area of his or her life, no grounds for compulsory action would exist other than taking the parents to court for prosecution. This, in itself, may do nothing to change the child's behaviour and may even reinforce it by appearing to blame their parents for the problem.

Plugging the gaps

There are undoubtedly children who fall through the net. In theory services are available to help such a family, and they should be offered by all agencies. But a child may refuse to cooperate with them and other agencies will not see their role as enforcing a particular kind of behaviour on a young person now considered able to take some responsibility for their own lives, even before the age of 16, even if parents and authorities do not agree with what they are doing.

We shall come back later to the crucial issue that perhaps British society on the eve of the 21st century can no longer expect its younger citizens simply to do as they are told when it comes to going to school. There can be no going back to some past age when they did not know what they know now and were seen but not heard. Many young people of 14 or 15 are successfully living an 'adult' lifestyle whether we like it or not. Perhaps we need new laws based on opportunity and entitlement rather than enforcement and punishment because, in reality, the law as it now stands is of little or no help in dealing with the difficulties presented by those with the greatest problem.

A step in a *more* punitive direction, while possible, would be, to all intents and purposes, unenforceable. Is it seriously suggested that the police and EWOs/ESWs should have the power to go into people's homes and drag their children kicking and screaming to school? What would happen when we got the child there? What would detaining children on the streets do to undermine all that has been said about not going with strangers? What opportunities might it present to those trying to pose as bogus officers? If there are to be new laws they would need to be imaginative and realistic. Just fining more parents or a return to imposing greater sanctions against children (which can only mean separating more of them from their families), will only make the situation worse.

REFERENCES

DfE/WO (1992) *Choice and Diversity – A new framework for schools*, London: HMSO

Family Law Reports (No. 1) (1993) Judgement of Judge Douglas Brown in the Family Division in the case of Essex CC v.B, 11.11.92, p.866 ff.

Solihull LEA (1991) *Report to the Education Sub-Committee*, 30 December.

Whitney, B (1993) *The Children Act and Schools*, London: Kogan Page

3

Truancy, Tables and the Truth

DEFINITIONS

It is impossible to say how much truancy there is in England and Wales today. We do not know if it is increasing or decreasing, even within individual schools. Any survey will quote a different figure, depending entirely on what is being studied and the definitions used. 'Truancy' is often ill-defined and covers only some of the circumstances in which children are absent from school without excuse; the word is frequently used when another term would be better. Consequently no one can claim to have established a definitive measure of the problem. When people start in different places, it is no surprise that they end up with different conclusions.

At least four concepts are currently in circulation, each of which adds something to the overall picture, none of which can be used in isolation.

Unauthorized absence

This is the term defined by the Department for Education in the 1991 Regulations as the basis of the 'truancy' tables published from 1993 (now more properly called 'absence tables'). These show *all* those absences which have not been authorized by the school, ie, for which 'leave' has not been given or no other valid explanation has been provided. As schools apply widely differing criteria, and there can be significant variation even within schools, this definition is open to considerable interpretation, despite attempts by the DfE to standardize practice.

There is no guarantee that the figures in the league tables are comparing like with like – some schools are very strict in their definition of authorized absence, others much more generous. Actual levels of attendance and absence between any two given schools may be identical even though their league-table figures may vary significantly. We cannot tell whether this discrepancy actually reflects the reality; we only know what percentage of their total possible attendance the school judges to be unauthorized absence. Reasons for such absences being recorded range from incompetence upwards:

- lost notes (either by child or school);
- inefficient record-keeping by class tutors/secretaries;
- valid absences which parents forgot to account for;
- holidays taken by parents without prior approval;
- strict definitions of 'late';
- absence without parents' knowledge;
- parents deliberately keeping children at home;
- children working illegally during the day;
- children who have simply stopped coming, against their parents' wishes.

The first sets of published tables did not tell us how many absences were authorized by the school, though they will do so in future. This is only a partial improvement however; the grounds on which authorization was given also need to be made clear. It would, for example, tend to penalize the school which uses outside resources, link courses, special units, etc., as these would still have to be declared as absences. It will also cause problems for schools with large ethnic minority communities where extended visits abroad would also have to be declared (unless children are taken off roll as suggested in Chapter 2).

On this measure, the 1993 tables revealed an average figure of 1 per cent of possible attendances being accounted for by unauthorized absences. A total of 12 per cent of pupils were said to have had at least one such absence (out of a school year of approximately 390 sessions), though this element has now been dropped from the published tables. Only one half-day unexplained was sufficient to be included in the statistics but this system takes no account of all the children who may have been marked present but who did not remain in school for the whole session.

Neither did the 12 per cent distinguish between pupils who were frequently or even permanently absent and those who just missed the odd day without proper explanation; they each counted as one towards the total. With most schools reporting figures of less than half of 1 per cent of sessions missed, and many claiming none at all, there is little ground for national concern here, except for those schools reporting the highest figures. Many of those, however, will claim that they have been much more diligent in their record-keeping or that it is unfair to compare a school which has to take all-comers from a given neighbourhood with those which can select their intake by ability or other criteria. In the judgement of many observers, these figures leave us with far more questions than answers.

Truancy

This has several definitions but focuses around action by *children* in choosing not to participate in the school day. Not all 'unau-thorised absence' is truancy (if the parent has deliberately kept the child away from school), and not all 'truancy' is likely to be recor-ded as unauthorized absence (if the child leaves lessons/school after registration). Different studies use different criteria but it is now generally recognized as helpful to distinguish between tru-ancy for whole sessions or days and that which involves only missing individual lessons or parts of sessions. In this case, truancy can happen even if the child never actually leaves the school premises.

Despite the misleading language used by many about what these children are doing, neither kind of truancy is illegal, not at any rate as far as the child is concerned. Children cannot break the law and there is no law which can be used to prosecute them. Truancy is not the same as shoplifting or stealing cars. If the root cause of the problem is illegal action by *parents*, it is not helpful to describe this as truancy. Truancy is behaviour within the child's control. It is primarily a disciplinary issue, not a matter of law enforcement. It is quite common (I did it myself) and there is much that can be done by schools to detect and prevent it.

Truancy could even be seen as an entirely normal reaction to something which the child finds boring or unpleasant; a rational avoidance, like 'forgetting' your dentist appointment or ringing in sick when you have a difficult meeting ahead. Most children grow out of it, though some develop a habit which is hard to break and, for a while, it may have a serious effect on their education. Many simply grow tired of school and decide that other ways of spending their time are more interesting. But many emerge unscathed and may even go on into further education at school or college, especially in the current climate of very limited employment opportunities.

School refusal

This is quite different, and much more difficult to deal with. Such absences could be seen by a school as either authorized or unauthorized depending on the circumstances, though the labelling may be rather arbitrary and greatly influenced by judgements about 'deserving' and 'undeserving' cases. These children don't just truant; they refuse school for weeks or months at a time. They are unpersuaded by all the efforts of parents, teachers and agencies, or they will only return to school after long and arduous attempts to change their minds. Sometimes the term 'school phobic' is used for some of them, though on the whole this is unhelpful as the root cause of their behaviour is not usually anything to do with school at all. It is just that they have chosen absence from school as the way in which to express themselves.

At the margins there will be some improvements where schools can offer flexible or part-time arrangements; some children will be more at home in special schools or small units (though these are increasingly difficult to resource and often only mainstream schools are on offer). Some will cooperate only with tuition at home where it is available. These children may be angry, confused, depressed or anxious; they may have major emotional and behavioural problems or be the victims of abuse; they may have developed an 'adult' lifestyle in which school attendance is no longer conceivable; they may be 'beyond parental control' or 'looked after' by the local authority. The reasons for their refusal to attend may be many and varied, but the resultant behaviour is only very occasional attendance or literally none at all.

These are the children who will primarily occupy the caseloads of EWOs/ESWs, rather than the true 'truants' who will normally be much more responsive to conventional disciplinary and monitoring procedures within the school. No new technology or stricter regime will influence these children. They know that they cannot be forced to go to school against their will or, in many cases, it is agreed by everyone that they should not be put under pressure to do so for the time being.

Some of them might be suitable for an education supervision order under the Children Act 1989 as a means of promoting their welfare. Some will be unable to form any effective relationships with adults and will be entirely unaffected by meetings, orders or courts. Some will simply drift out of education from about 14 and there will be nothing anyone can do about it. There is no way of knowing exactly how many of them there are, but any neighbourhood high school can expect to have some, probably scattered across the age-range with a concentration in Years 10 and 11. In some areas, especially cities, there will be unknown numbers of such children who have simply 'disappeared' from the education system.

Condoned absence

These children are absent because of failure by their parents to fulfil their legal duty or with the tacit approval of either parents or school. They are working in the family business, moving around the country, looking after sick relatives or younger children, exploiting their parents' lack of interest in education, or at home 'cooling off' after an incident at school. In many of these families a culture of non-attendance has developed in which all the structures, rewards and sanctions promote absence rather than attendance.

The parents may rightly be subject to the pressure of prosecution where they have persistently failed to act appropriately, though some absence is condoned only because there is no hope of changing the situation. Where support services to help the family are not available, children and parents may have no choice but to juggle their commitments and the children attend school only as often as is realistically possible.

Where these absences are being condoned by schools, this may be because there is sympathy for the child's plight or, in other circumstances, because it suits the school for the child not to attend. Some children may be advised not to come in for a while or are awaiting possible admission to an alternative school. For many teachers, parents and children this will be seen as preferable to formal exclusion.

Other definitions

These categories are not, of course, mutually exclusive; some children will move from one to another over a period of time. Occasional truancy may lead to significant school refusal; what begins with parents keeping a child at home may lead to the child exploiting the lack of boundaries or finding it very difficult to return. But different writers on the subject have aimed to make similar distinctions in order to do justice to the range of issues involved. In a reader edited by Ken Reid (one of the key writers on truancy during the 1980s), Stephen Murgatroyd gives a slightly different and wider meaning to the word 'truancy' and applies it to a variety of contexts, described below (1987, p.123).

Telic truancy

This is essentially focused around anxiety and occurs when children find the school experience and its environment over-arousing. Such factors as the timetable, changes in location, feelings of under-achievement or examination pressure lead these children to avoid the stress of school by not attending. Typically this behaviour also causes anxiety in itself; the child then worries about missing school and its consequences. The more pressure they are placed under, the more anxious they become and the less able they are to stop it.

Paratelic truancy

This is the exact opposite. These children are sensation-seeking rather than trying to avoid it. They enjoy the experience, even the thrill of being absent from school. They relish the attention which it brings them and the consequent challenge to the authority of either parents or professionals. The more attention they are given, the more exciting and attractive the truancy becomes. They will be brazen about their behaviour and, unlike the telic truants, will not be afraid to be seen out and about when they should be at school. These children are more likely to be seen as 'bad' as distinct from the rather 'sad' figure often cut by the telic truants.

Conformist truancy

These children truant because others do it; they are responding to some group or peer pressure within their gang or culture. They may follow the leadership of the paratelic truants, but they do not show the same self-confident defiance when away from the group. They swing between telic and paratelic behaviour and will be relatively responsive to attempts to change them, especially when separated from the group. They may lack self-confidence and with greater self-esteem may choose not to be so subject to the pressure of others. Some will be conforming to parental pressure rather than pressure from peers, where, for example, parents are dependent on them for practical help or household tasks and seek to persuade the child to remain at home in either subtle or overt ways.

Negativistic truancy

This involves the deliberate rejection of pressure to conform, the opposite of conformist truancy. Here the pressure, whether per-ceived or real, is from parents and teachers to be successful. In response to this pressure, the child does the complete opposite and rejects the expected behaviour by absenting themselves from school. This may be about trying to demonstrate power within the family or group (mastery negativism), or it may be intended to invoke sympathy (sympathy negativism). Often there is an unresolved conflict of some kind, with either a parent or teacher.

As is obvious from such an approach, Murgatroyd is strongly committed to the counselling method for resolving children's problems, with the emphasis on identifying underlying causes which must be addressed by individual and group therapeutic processes. Others see different kinds of truancy in more descriptive terms, such as the distinctions drawn by Holmes (1989, p.10), given below.

Opportunistic truancy

This refers to the occasional truants who just take time off when they feel like it, or when some other alternative is available. They will skip school when the fair is in town or when there is something else more fun to do, but otherwise they attend regularly.

Subsistence truancy

This applies to the descendants of the 19th century children who were too poor for school. They may literally lack the necessary shoes and clothes to attend. Holmes also calls it 'domestic truancy' where children are needed to maintain the family economy either through work or, more commonly, helping out with other children while the parents go to work.

Habitual truancy

This covers children for whom the behaviour has become more than just an occasional escape. They have developed a way of life which includes regular time away from school. This might be the same day each week or a regular on-off pattern over a number of weeks or months. They ignore school for significant amounts of time, though they may not have much else to do as an alternative.

Retreatist truancy

This may be more unconscious, indicative of deep-seated feelings and impervious to normal threats, reprisals or incentives. These children have given up school and there is little or no prospect of their returning. Some may lead deliberately isolated lifestyles, away from normal relationships with peers and adults. Some may seek intense and even sexual commitment to one person and see themselves as too 'grown-up' for school.

A typology of absence

To gain the complete picture, it is necessary to develop a very sophisticated typology such as that given by Carlen *et al* (1992, p.62 ff). In each case, I have indicated whether or not these absences are likely to be authorized under current regulations.

Officially induced (authorized)
Absences due to action by the school; formal exclusions, closures due to industrial action, health and safety problems, heating failures, etc. Classes sent home due to shortages of teachers. Informal 'suspensions' and disputes over discipline (eg, uniform, behaviour and broken 'contracts').

Officially approved (authorized)
Leave given due to sickness, approved holidays, pregnancy, study leave, licensed performances etc.

Officially illicit but unofficially condoned (authorized)
Children given unofficial permission to be absent or whose absences are accepted as inevitable and about which nothing can be done. Children who have a history of disruption or who are so far behind in their coursework that there is little point in their being at school. (These absences are not likely to be referred for any further action.)

Officially illicit but parentally approved (unauthorized)
Children who are absent with the support of their parents. If they have provided apparently satisfactory explanations, absences might be authorized, at least to start with. But where a school exercises careful vigilance and reasons have been found to be spurious, or no reason has been given, they should be left unauthorized. These parents are likely to be seen as committing an offence.

Officially illicit but parentally condoned (often authorized)
Children whose behaviour is causing concern but where parents have given up, even though they accept they should be at school. 'Looked after' children who refuse to attend. Some might need alternative provision but none is available and parents do not feel it is right to require them to attend in the meantime. Some of these absences might result in prosecution (if the school does not authorize them) or in education supervision orders.

Officially illicit but parentally disapproved (unauthorized)
Absences which should not be authorized but about which it may be difficult to do very much other than patient negotiation/other provision. Parents cannot be held responsible, even though the absences are unauthorized; they are cooperating fully but are powerless. There will be a temptation to authorize the absences on the grounds that they have at least been explained, but this would not be correct. An education supervision order might be appropriate in some cases, though it will often be held that there is little chance of success.

Internal and illicit (probably marked present)
Children who attend for registration and so are not absent at all, though they fail to turn up for part sessions or lessons. No offence by parents could be upheld and grounds for an education supervision order would be difficult to establish. Children who arrive late as well as avoiding some lessons would have to be marked absent, then present, then missing!

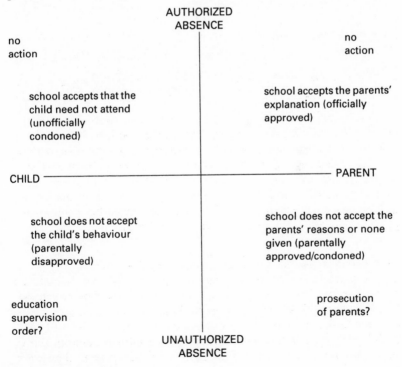

Figure 3.1 *Absence grid*

It is therefore possible to plot these various forms of absence according to two criteria: authorized/unauthorized and whether the child or the parent may be held primarily responsible (see Figure 3.1). Whether or not the absence becomes defined as a problem depends on where it is placed on this grid. No action is likely if the school is satisfied with the explanations given and so authorizes the absence, or if the school itself is condoning the absence.

Truancy belongs only in the bottom left quadrant and, if any court proceedings become appropriate, it would be action under the Children Act 1989 for an education supervision order. Only in the bottom right quadrant would it be appropriate to consider the prosecution of parents. (Absence after registration, which would also be properly included in the word 'truancy', does not feature on this grid as, legally speaking, it is not likely to be defined as absence, though a court *might* be prepared to consider it as part of a wider picture in ESO proceedings.)

THE TRUANCY UNIT STUDY

A school-centred approach

The previous section is intended to make it clear that much talk of 'truancy' is misplaced and that truancy is only a part of the problem. Indeed, it may be by far the easiest part to deal with. This is why I would want to treat with some caution the findings of the most widely-publicized study in recent years. This research (O'Keeffe and Stoll, 1994), undertaken by the Truancy Unit at the University of North London and commissioned and promoted by the Department for Education, has rightly been hailed as the most thorough investigation for some time.

Thirty-eight thousand pupils in the final two years of compulsory education at 150 schools in 20 LEAs were surveyed through the completion of confidential questionnaires. The two key features of this report are:

1. its very wide definition of truancy as including occasions when the child attends for most of the day but misses odd lessons, *even if they do not leave the school premises* (post-registration truancy), as well as whole-session absenteeism (blanket truancy); and,
2. its insistence that the primary cause of truancy, in both forms, lies within the school rather than in the background or home circumstances of the child. Schools in similar areas of depri-

vation had widely varying rates of truancy. The study also found little or no evidence for a link between truancy and crime (despite the claims often made to the contrary).

With such a wide definition it is not surprising that figures well in excess of those reported as 'unauthorized absence' were revealed: 30 per cent of respondents admitted to at least some truancy, with post-registration truancy the more common. There was little difference between boys and girls, though girls predominated in Y10 and boys in Y11. As any informed observer would expect, truancy is more common in Y11 (36 per cent) than in Y10 (25 per cent). Even though there is more post-registration truancy than blanket truancy, most truants do both. About half said that their parents knew about the truancy, though it is not clear whether they also condoned it.

When asked the reasons for their absenteeism, most laid the blame on the school: irrelevant lessons (36 per cent), dislike of teacher (29 per cent), dislike of subject (21 per cent), and coursework problems (19 per cent) were the most common explanations. Maths was the most unpopular lesson, closely followed by English and PE/games (an interesting contribution to the debate about compulsory team sports). Technology had the lowest rate of absence. The researchers make much of the fact that the children rarely, if ever, referred to reasons outside the school or to many of the more 'fashionable' explanations such as bullying (2 per cent) or racism (not even mentioned).

Implications for EWOs

The authors are keen to stress the significance of this for those professionally involved with children who do not attend:

EWOs need not abandon their long term interest in children for whom school is difficult and threatening because of their troubled home background etc. There always have been such children and there always will be presumably. What EWOs will need to do in the light of current reorganisation of ancillary educational services, however, is to show a greater interest than before in 'mainstream' truancy. By mainstream truancy may be understood that truancy which recent evidence shows to have its origin mainly in dissatisfaction with lessons, i.e. the truancy in question has a rational and pondered basis. Rejection of lessons is not the only reason for truancy; but it is by far the most important (O'Keeffe, 1993, p.4).

I suspect that EWOs/ESWs have known for some time that many of their clients were dissatisfied with their lessons! But the researchers are right to remind us that truancy, *according to their definition*, is largely a 'normal' phenomenon engaged in by 'normal' children. Such behaviour can be dealt with by concerted action by schools and parents with, where resources permit, help from outside agencies. As will be explored in the next chapter, schools must recognize that many of the answers to truancy of this kind lie within their hands and that a great deal can be done to detect, prevent and discourage such behaviour. This is a hopeful and realistic emphasis.

However, we should not be deluded into thinking that this will resolve all the problems. There appears to be a particular concern in this research to play down what might be seen as 'social work' approaches to absence from school in favour of responses based on greater vigilance and internal school-based action:

> When pupils were asked to write freely about the reasons for cutting lessons or truanting from school if they did so, a minority of truants mentioned home difficulties. If a concentration on home difficulties has constituted a major element in the work of EWOs to date, then the concentration may have been wrong, but not the idea itself.... The point in need of emphasis is that in most cases truants' answers do not suggest a pathological deficiency in the children themselves ... if there is a pathology in relation to truancy it may be more readily sought in the curriculum than in the personalities of children. (ibid, pp.5–6)

Reservations

No one could quarrel with the suggestion that much can be done to make school a more attractive environment for children to come to, including changes to the curriculum, more stimulating teaching, better pastoral systems and tackling the feeling that some children have that they are not particularly welcome when they do come. But placing too much emphasis on this carries certain dangers. I would want to make three particular points in response.

First, this survey did not include those children who have the most serious problem with absenteeism. It is, by definition, a study only of those children who truant from time to time but who were at school to complete the questionnaires. No work was done with children while they were out of school. The persistent school refusers were not there when the exercise was carried out – some of the 7,000 children who were absent to whom the researchers refer.

This must make us extremely cautious about seeing this research as identifying the reasons for *their* behaviour. It is best to be very clear that this is a study into truancy, as defined by the researchers and particularly into post-registration truancy.

It tells us little or nothing about those children who cause most concern and whose problems are most difficult to resolve. It seems to me inevitable that it will be these children who will most occupy the time and expertise of the welfare professionals. If they are to spend more time with the 'mainstream' truants there would need to be considerably more of them, and who will work with the chronic refusers whom schools have no opportunity to influence?

Second, children are not likely to refer to family difficulties in the context of a survey which is obviously about school, completed at school and with no involvement by parents. Few young people would see this as the place to refer to confidential details about their family life, even assuming they were able to understand and articulate their difficulties with school attendance in that way. As the authors of the report acknowledge, children who give a super-ficial explanation in this context might well reveal deeper causes when asked to explore them in a safe, more personal encounter with a skilled worker.

Third, it must also be recognized that such a definition of the problem has major implications for the local management of schools. If the evidence of the research is that the primary place where change is needed is within the school, this must be reflected in the way in which governors and headteachers define their priorities. Pastoral specialists are becoming a rarity and those that there are seem to have decreasing opportunity to spend time away from the classroom. Teachers are not social workers or counsellors; most of them are not trained at all in how to deal with the problems of individual pupils. Too much emphasis on action by the school in isolation may marginalize work with vulnerable young people where it should be opened up to inter-agency practice in which a range of skills and resources is available.

I greatly welcome this piece of research, but I am suspicious of its intentions (or of the way in which it may be used to scale down education social work provision) and of the fact that it is being seen as 'official' and therefore more valid than other approaches. If its implications were followed through it would need a far greater commitment by the DfE to helping schools to improve their educational product rather than simply imposing dubious measurements of statistical performance. It gives children and young people a voice, always a useful idea. But is anyone listening to their complaints? All the signs are that little is going to change as a result. If it leads only to more lectures on trying harder, with no recognition of the need for more fundamental changes, it will have little impact on children's behaviour. If it fosters a climate in which their wider needs are seen as irrelevant to their education, it will be a disaster.

RESPONSES AND PRIORITIES

'Truancy Watch'

The way in which we define the problem is very important when deciding how best to respond. Ideas such as 'Truancy Watch' (as promoted by the DfE) or patrols in shopping centres, etc. rest on certain assumptions about what is going on. They have their place – though there are serious questions about whether they represent a good use of scarce resources in all but a very few places where there is clear evidence of a significant need. EWOs/ESWs have better things to do than simply hang about town centres on the off-chance. Such programmes must be very carefully monitored and evaluated and have a clear 'welfare' or 'partnership' approach, with no element of intimidation or threat – features of the widely-publicized Staffordshire scheme which are often overlooked by those interpreting it as something else.

Such initiatives are probably only of much value when children are clearly at risk or when parents with children are approached on the grounds that they might at least be reasonably expected to explain why their child is not at school. This all helps to maintain the profile of education and can be a positive sign of the community's care for its young people. It may also have some effect on juvenile crime figures, though this may not be sustained for long, or the crimes may simply be committed elsewhere.

But if the reasons for absence are more complicated, these time-consuming and potentially conflict-ridden tactics will be of very limited relevance. Many children identified in this way will already be well-known absentees. This approach would have no impact at all on those who are determined to avoid detection, who are spending their time at home or whose family life is in serious difficulty.

If EWOs/ESWs are to spend more time on the visible and 'mainstream' truants, what will happen to those parents and children who will be quite untouched by such activities? Detecting children is one thing; some will give up when they are found out.

But for many, returning them to school, making sure that they stay there and, most importantly of all, helping them actually to receive some benefit from their education, will all require much more thorough and individual responses. The suggestion that by catching them we have resolved their problems will simply not be true for many.

Meeting children's needs

There seems to be a common assumption in much of the current concern about truancy that by collecting data we will change behaviour; that schools, parents and children will all do better once the game is up. Headteachers are increasingly concerned that action should be taken to deal with the rows of empty noughts in the register, which may reflect badly on the school once the league table figure is published. Where the absence is directly related to internal school practice, the new emphasis on accounting for absences can usefully draw attention to the child who is developing a problem so that action can be taken. Any system which picks up children quickly so that difficulties can be nipped in the bud is to be welcomed.

But many children's needs are not being met by this procedure. The school's primary aim may be to reduce the figures; it is on this that they will be judged, not on how much effort they have made to deal with the root causes. As long as the absences can be authorized there can appear to be no reason for concern. If the school does not feel that the causes are within its control, or if there is nothing that can immediately be done to improve the situation, many head-teachers will be happy to authorize the absences rather than risk being seen to have a problem. The odd nought for the occasional truant might disappear altogether so that the pupil need not feature at all in the statistics. A whole string of absences might be author-ized on the grounds that they have been explained by the EWO/ESW as school refusal or condoned absence.

A new defensiveness

It may even be that the introduction of authorized and unauthorized absences has made the situation worse. It has focused attention away from levels of *attendance* which are a far more neutral measure than the percentage of the absences which the school judges to be illicit. It has made it more difficult to collect evidence against those parents who are genuinely failing in their duty as the school may be reluctant to leave absences unauthorized or to establish tighter arrangements with parents about the provision of notes, etc. More time and energy now goes into collecting, presenting and even manipulating the figures that in actually getting to grips with why the child is absent and what can be done about it.

It is not that schools are being deliberately deceitful, though I have come across plenty of examples of very generous definitions of 'leave', well beyond the grounds envisaged by the regulations. It is more that they have now become so defensive about their levels of absence, desperate to appear more popular with their pupils or better-run than the school down the road and so less willing to persist with the child who will bring them little credit. There is little for a school to shout about if it manages to help a child increase their attendance from 20 to 70 per cent, but that might represent a monumental achievement by all concerned. In the league table it still looks like failure.

Headteachers will now exclude children for non-attendance – perhaps the maddest sanction ever conceived – but one that is inevitable if a school is unwilling to allow the child to ruin their statistics. A system intended to encourage schools to do better may actually be having the opposite effect, because most have started from such a negligible percentage of unauthorized absence. They are desperate not to do worse and will do almost anything to make sure that this year's figure is no higher than last year's.

Not all problems with school attendance are capable of immediate resolution. Everyone seems to want a 'quick fix' brought about by instant action. Once you move away from just calling it all 'truancy' and expecting LEAs to 'crack down' on it, it is obvious that a much more sophisticated response is involved, according to exactly what it is we are dealing with. Any school serving an average group of children must expect to have some who will not attend all the time. Only by selecting your intake and removing all those who don't comply can a school genuinely produce an unauthorized absence figure of 0 per cent. Most schools cannot be in that favoured position if we are to avoid large numbers of children unwanted by any school and left to fend for themselves – a phenomenon which is a very real possibility everywhere and a present reality in some places.

Thinking positively

This quest for perfection is simply not realistic and is putting some schools, children and parents under tremendous pressure. Everyone needs to relax a bit. The truth about truancy is that the over-whelming majority of children attend school with remarkably little difficulty. It is tremendously encouraging that even those who skip school now and then still like it most of the time and suffer no lasting ill-effects. Many return for further study after the minimum leaving age when they have had a bit more time to grow up and think about their future. This is all excellent testimony to the quality of our schools and the commitment of our children. But any expectation that we can eliminate all signs of teenage rebellion and turn our schools into havens of learning where all the children always do as they are told is clearly impossible.

A bit less emphasis on failure and a bit more talk about all the things that can be done and are being done by schools, children, parents and LEAs *together*, to help the small minority with a real problem, would be most welcome. Punitive noises, superficial comparisons and simplistic solutions will not help us. Careful, flexible and thoughtful analysis, based on a thorough assessment of children's needs, with the necessary resources then being made available to meet them, will take us forward where no league table ever will.

REFERENCES

Carlen, P, Gleeson, D and Wardhaugh, J (1992) *Truancy – The Politics of Compulsory Schooling*, Buckingham: Open University Press.

Holmes, G (1989) *Truancy and Social Welfare*, Cheadle: Boys and Girls Welfare Society

O'Keeffe, D (1993) 'Truancy in English secondary schools', *The Education Social Worker*, 225, December.

O'Keeffe, D and Stoll, P (1994) *Truancy in English Secondary Schools*, London: HMSO.

Reid, K (ed.) (1987) *Combating School Absenteeism*, Sevenoaks: Hodder and Stoughton.

4

Whole-school Policies

EVALUATING CURRENT PRACTICE

A change of mood?

The exposure to more public scrutiny of rates of unauthorized absence has required all schools to become more accountable for their performance in this area. This must be a good thing. One of the key management functions in any school must be a determined attempt to ensure that educational opportunity is offered to all pupils according to 'their age, ability and aptitude and any special educational needs they may have'. This can't happen if they're not there. The first priority of any governing body and teaching staff is to do their best to make sure children attend.

The fact that the concept of 'unauthorized' absence was imposed with little or no consultation in advance and the inherent weaknesses in the league table concept, have made some schools resentful and suspicious of the whole idea. A few have even refused to participate in the exercise at all or have been distinctly half-hearted, producing figures which owe more to creative accounting than actual performance. There are very reasonable grounds for this scepticism, especially if your school is unable to control its admissions, has to try and serve a wide variety of children or is facing false comparison with those who start from somewhere entirely different.

However, I believe that the government is right when it maintains that this reluctance is sometimes a symptom of a deeper malaise. Perhaps there was something approaching a fatalistic attitude around in the 1980s: that if your school served a community beset by social difficulties, it was inevitable that levels of attendance would be poor. Perhaps this tended to lead everyone – teachers, governors, parents and children – to feel that there was not much point in bothering. Many staff found it easier to pull up the drawbridge and keep the problems at bay by indifference and even a certain hostility. It is not so long ago that a school of my acquaintance had a notice on its main doors reading 'No Entry for Parents'!

Breaking the cycle
The characteristic of such situations was a cycle of blame. The parents blamed the school for being distant and elitist, no doubt fuelled by unhappy memories of their own education. The governors blamed the parents for not bothering and not giving school a very high priority in their lives. Teachers blamed children for being lazy and uninterested while children blamed teachers for not understanding them and teaching only irrelevant things they didn't need to know.

The headteacher blamed the LEA for not doing enough to remind parents of their responsibilities or for not showing enough interest in the school; the LEA blamed the headteacher and the governors for failing to build proper relationships and create an attractive and accepting environment. All the professionals involved, EWOs/ ESWs, teachers, social workers, psychologists, etc. blamed each other – and when all else failed, they blamed the parents again, the only people with any statutory duty who could be made to answer before a court for their failure. (This professional buck-passing is well-described by Carlen *et al.*, 1992, p.89 ff.) I put all this in the past tense which may be rather foolish. But a number of things have happened which should be changing the mood about school attendance, if not yet completely then at least in part.

First, schools have had to come to terms with a new relationship with parents: they can no longer be only shadowy figures who belong outside the gates. This is something of an uncertain concept, with many of the traditional ways in which parents are supposed to be involved still struggling to survive. Annual meetings, PTAs and governor ballots might only attract a minute percentage of the total electorate, but the principle is being established. Schools are trying to give new thought to more imaginative and flexible ways of enabling parents to participate when there are problems; many barriers are coming down; new models of partnership are emerging. Many will feel they have been thrown into these relationships without necessarily saying that they wanted them, but everyone is having to at least make some effort to make them work.

Second, professionals are having to seek new ways of working together, particularly since the Children Act 1989 became law in

1991. The working practices which the Act has encouraged have all been based around a model of inter-agency provision rather than each adopting a narrow perspective of their own. This has not, of course, been universally successful and has been promoted far less by the Department for Education than I would wish, but now that children with attendance difficulties or who are excluded from school will be seen by local authorities as 'children in need', the basic structures have been put in place. The code of practice for special educational needs, arising from the Education Act 1993 and undoubtedly one of the better documents of recent years, has encouraged this process even further, as do the necessary working relationships required for child protection and education super-vision orders. Education is operating less in isolation, which must be a good thing.

Third, with the widespread implementation of local financial management and the advent of performance tables, the responsi-bility more clearly lies at the local school level than it used to. This gives the school much greater freedom to use its initiative and begin to tackle its own problems without feeling dependent on the LEA to do it for them. Even those who have grave doubts about going the whole way towards grant maintained status would not want to go back to a point where this sense of local responsibility was often in conflict with the central planners. But with more control over resources must come acceptance of new roles, previously delegated to 'them' at County Hall, even allowing for the fact that the 'bottom line' responsibility on attendance still lies with the LEA.

Checklists for action

As a consequence, bearing in mind that levels of absence and the quality of whole-school attendance policies have been clearly identified as part of the new OFSTED inspection process, there has never been a better time for schools to review their commitment to these issues. This has been forced upon them by the 1991 Pupils' Attendance Regulations and by new guidance from the Department for Education (DfE, May 1994) which has spelt out clearly the government's expectations for day-to-day practice.

All schools have a primary duty to report to the LEA on children who are continually absent for two weeks without explanation or whose attendance gives cause for concern over a period of time (Regulation 7 of the Pupils' Registration Regulations 1956). Schools retain an accountability to the LEA in this area where other obligations have long since disappeared. One aim of this chapter is to offer a range of issues through which a governing body might wish to work in order to review its procedures and establish that its practice meets the legal requirements.

Whole-school commitment to dealing effectively with absence undoubtedly begins with the headteacher and the governors. Children, parents and staff will not be able to work together unless there is clear leadership from within the senior management team. These are issues of policy just as much as practice. A number of writers have identified checklists which enable school managers to ensure that they have addressed the necessary issues. Leadership by senior staff always features, as in this helpful list of factors which promote attendance identified by Bayliss in the *Times Educational Supplement*, April 1986 (quoted in Reid, 1987, p.10):

- purposeful leadership of the staff by the head;
- involvement of the deputy head(s);
- involvement of teachers;
- consistency amongst teachers;
- a structured day;
- intellectually challenging teaching;
- a work-centred environment;
- a limited focus within sessions;
- maximum communication between teachers and pupils;
- thorough record-keeping;
- parental involvement;
- a positive climate.

The Hargreaves Report, *Improving Secondary Schools*, published in 1984, identified the following practical steps towards improving attendance, many of which were also taken up by the Elton Report, *Discipline in Schools*, in 1989:

- a senior teacher charged with specific responsibility for pupil attendance;
- a list of absentees being produced quickly, ideally by morning break, for use by appropriate office and teaching staff;
- the school devising a sensitive scheme for the immediate follow-up of absentees – for example either by telephoning home or sending out letters to parents;
- form tutors ensuring that records of attendance are as accurate as possible and explanations for absence are produced when pupils return to school;
- heads of year/house monitoring the work of form tutors;

- heads of year/house and teachers with responsibility for pupil attendance having regular meetings with EWOs;
- regular 'spot-checks' for specific-lesson truancy and for pupils leaving school before the end of the day;
- rewards for individual pupils or classes with an excellent attendance record, in the form of praise or prizes;
- penalties for pupils who are consistently late;
- absentees and truants being quietly welcomed back on their return to school and efforts being made to re-integrate them socially and academically. (Reid, 1987, p.203)

Putting it into practice

All of this will, of course, be stunningly obvious to the seasoned teacher though, even with the best of intentions, it may not always be carried out in practice. It is perhaps too easy to say that these things are done automatically, without actually checking whether this is true. Computerization, for example, has made the collecting of information about absence much easier, but there will still be significant breakdowns in procedures if tutors are sloppy about registration or fail to act on the information obtained.

Indeed there is a danger that under such systems staff may feel that attendance has become an administrative rather than a pastoral issue, unless the technology is used appropriately. Even the best-run system may not actually be working towards the promotion of attendance, no matter how efficiently the data are being recorded. (Some schools are already abandoning computerized registration on these grounds.)

Or, to pick up another example from this list, teachers do not always appreciate just how difficult it may be for children to return after a long absence and too many pupils tell stories of being made to feel embarrassed and self-conscious for some of them at least not to be true. It will be for governors and senior managers to establish that good practice is being carried out in the face of the very real pressures from all the other things which are competing for staff's attention.

A range of strategies

The HMI report, *Attendance at School* (HMI, 1989), one of the first official documents to talk about 'justified' and 'unjustified' absence, contains a valuable list of proven strategies (p.23):

- sending letters to parents of new pupils after the first 100 possible attendances with special praise both for those with 100% attendance and those with no avoidable absences;

- awarding certificates for punctuality and attendance;
- holding inter-class, or inter-house, competitions for the best or most markedly improved attendance;
- recording attendance on reports sent home (now required), with positive comments for effort;
- entering improvements on the school record of a poor attender;
- sending children to senior members of staff for commendation of efforts made towards improvement, as well as for full attendance;
- setting up a sub-committee of governors to meet with poor attenders and encourage them to return at a later date to talk about improvements;
- identifying children 'at risk' before they transfer to another class or group or school, and devising ways of supporting them;
- including attendance-related matters in the induction pro-gramme for all new staff, especially for newly-qualified teachers;
- devising flexible and innovative responses to those who find it difficult to attend regularly for whatever reason;
- setting attainment goals for individuals or class or year groups;
- welcoming children back after illness;
- taking specific measures to ease children back into school after protracted absence;
- briefing teachers on how to organise the work of a class to allow for returning absentees without loss of momentum for the class as a whole.

These are all helpful and realistic ideas; no school will already be doing all of them. Again, careful scrutiny may reveal new opportunities. I particularly like the emphasis on rewarding those children whose attendance may not have reached 100 per cent but who have made considerable progress from a previously poor figure. Some children will never attend full-time but could do much better than they are currently managing. Reward systems often tend to reward the same children every time or offer only impossible targets in the eyes of some pupils; there must be as much recognition of effort as of achievement.

Many newly-qualified staff will have had little or no preparation for their role as a form tutor. The amount of training on pastoral issues in general appears to be minimal, with new teachers often knowing nothing about child protection, the law on attendance or the keeping of registers. Yet these are amongst the people with front-line responsibility for monitoring and encouraging attendance and safeguarding children's welfare. Clear policy right from the beginning is especially important in this context.

Action by governors

Finally, in this section, the following checklist (for which I am indebted to my colleague Francis Luckcock) may also be helpful as a way for governors to monitor practice in their school:

- The governing body has made itself familiar with:
  - the most recent attendance regulations published by the Department for Education;
  - the most recent guidelines on attendance issued by the local education authority;
  - instructions given to school staff on registration procedures.
- The governing body has revised its policy on attendance to take account of recent legislation and circulars.
- The governing body has presented the school attendance figures in the school brochure, published the dates of the school year and given guidance to children and parents on authorized and unauthorized absence, lateness, registration procedures, family holidays and the action required by parents and the school when children are absent.
- The governors have arranged for the Education Welfare Officer for the school to meet new parents at the induction event.
- The governors have prepared a presentation on school attendance for the annual parents' meeting.
- The governors have received an annual report from the Education Welfare Officer indicating their level of involvement, achievements, court action and any specific issues which need attention.
- The governing body has appointed one of its members to have oversight of school attendance matters, who will report to the governing body on a termly basis, having conferred with school staff primarily responsible for collating data on attendance and pastoral care, together with the Education Welfare Officer. The appointee will speak for the governing body on attendance matters during school inspections and present data indicating patterns of attendance per class/year, comparative data, etc. They will also indicate goals and strategies for improvement.
- The governing body has been active in rewarding individual

pupils and class groups for good attendance or significant improvement.

- The governing body has outlined strategies for improving attendance in the school development plan.
- The governing body has had recent training on managing school attendance, and has made training available to staff.

THREE KEY AREAS

Registration

Three specific areas of school-based action will now be explored in more detail, beginning with the quality of pupil registration and good practice by the form teacher. Registration can often be a derisory and insignificant part of the school day, passed over as quickly as possible by staff and pupils alike as a routine chore. This immediately gives the wrong impression.

Legal requirements
It is important to be clear that registration at the *beginning* of each morning and afternoon session is a legal requirement, however often it may be done in addition to these times (Regulation 3 of the Pupils' Registration Regulations 1956). Some teachers delegate the marking of registers to a pupil, which is probably illegal; others, seeking to thwart post-registration truancy, mark the afternoon register at the end of the school day, but this must be in addition to marking it after lunch, not instead of it.

Registers are legal documents, whether kept manually or on computer, exact copies of which must be produced for evidence purposes in any legal action by the LEA. Manual registers must be kept in ink and any corrections clearly shown. They must be retained for a minimum of three years. Computerized registers must also show any changes and when they were made; a print-out must be made at least monthly and bound copies of the year's records kept for at least three years.

Registration done properly reminds pupils that attendance is important and that someone notices if they are not there. It provides an opportunity for the sharing of news or for chasing up missing notes. It establishes that by coming late, something significant has been missed. Schools are free to allow a 'reasonable' period for registration (normally held to be no more than half an hour), beyond which the pupil is technically absent, even if they attend for the rest of the session. It is often difficult to enforce this, however, as no school wants to give the impression that the child may as well not have come at all, but there is clearly a need to establish that lateness matters and *could* still be seen as unauthorized absence where it persists.

Whether or not registration is done by means of a computer, registers must contain a mark for *every* session the class or group meets. If the child is absent, and the absence has been authorized by the school, each nought should contain the appropriate code indicating the reason for authorization being given. *All noughts then left with no code are unauthorized.* (Codes should not be entered only in the first and last absence, as seems to be common). It is often necessary to enter a provisional mark pending more information. This is perfectly legal provided the mark is changed to a permanent record as soon as possible, ie, not at the end of the school year!

Suggested symbols
The DES circular 11/91, arising from the 1991 Regulations, offers the following list of standard symbols to show authorized absences, though LEAs were given freedom to devise their own, provided the necessary information is recorded and authorized and unauthorized absences are clearly distinguished:

B   receiving part-time or temporary education at an off-site unit or other than at the school where registered;
C   other circumstances (to be specified);
E   excluded (fixed or permanent pending confirmation by the governors);
H   annual family holiday (for which leave has been granted in advance);
I   attending interview;
M   medical/dental;
P   approved sporting activity;
R   day of religious observance;
S   study leave;
V   educational visit;
W   work experience.

I would argue that some of these should be counted as present for statistical purposes (B, I, P, S, V and W), as the child is still engaged in an educational activity, but simply away from the school. This would have avoided the unfortunate case in which a parent was prosecuted for absence because her child was attending a unit for dyslexics. If it is all right to call a day trip to Alton Towers an 'educational visit', I do not see why this brief absence caused any problem. Unfortunately, the regulations do tend to imply that attendance can take place only in schools.

As was mentioned in Chapter 3, it seems most unfair that these activities have to be treated as absences at all if they have been agreed by the school as part of the child's programme. This makes it impossible for some children to achieve full attendance and may discourage staff and governors from making use of imaginative alternatives which then have to be declared. The register does, of course, need to show that they are not on the premises in case of fire, etc. but that is rather different.

Symbols should not be a matter of individual discretion; the same system should be in use throughout the school and it should be closely monitored by senior staff. The system should be made clear to parents in school brochures, etc. As has already been seen, the decision over whether or not to authorize an absence is of crucial significance for assessing what action may be required, and this should not be subject to the whim of too many individuals. Best practice is for class tutors to seek advice from a senior member of staff with special responsibility for attendance matters if there is any doubt over the validity of an explanation or about how to deal with a particular circumstance. This ensures an element of quality control which is in everyone's interests – staff, parents and pupils.

When problems arise
Where staff feel that too many absences are being accounted for by notes from parents, or that reasons given are not satisfactory, action should be taken as a matter of urgency to try and meet parents in order to clarify appropriate boundaries for the future. It is difficult for parents to understand what is wrong if the school has apparently been authorizing the absences without question but is also calling in the EWO/ESW on the grounds that there is a problem. Parents need to understand that the school will not authorize absence just because some kind of explanation has been given. As the 1994 Circular on categorization of absence makes clear, schools only have power to authorize absences for reasons set out in the regulations (DfE, 1994). While there is an element of discretion over what to include as 'other circumstances', this should not extend to *any* explanation, however trivial.

Where there is doubt over what is happening, it is always best to agree special arrangements with parents *in writing* – for example, where a child is frequently absent for minor illnesses or family difficulties. This might mean the school accepting such an explanation for short periods (one or two days), but making it clear that longer absences will not be authorized unless some independent verification is produced that the child was unfit for school. The failure of such attempts would then lead to referral to the EWO/ESW.

It is not always possible for parents to produce a doctor's note (they may charge) and there is no legal obligation on GPs or parents to provide them. Both doctors and dentists may regard their relationship with a patient as confidential. But some situations are capable of a negotiated procedure by which the school can seek reasonable verification with the consent of the parents. School nurses may be able to liaise with practice nurses. Some GPs will be willing to make special arrangements, if not to pass on medical information then at least to indicate that they have seen the child and whether or not they have been judged unfit for school and, if so, for how long.

Many teachers may feel that such investigation is not appropriate, but this is an inevitable consequence of the whole concept of authorized and unauthorized absence. Decisions cannot be made without information. Sensitivity will sometimes be required and EWO/ESWs will be able to assist, though it is not primarily their responsibility. But however it is done, it is important not to send the signal that any explanation will do and that no effort at all will be made to detect an abuse of the system. No school can hope to deal effectively with attendance issues if it either denies the need for such procedures or fails to carry them out efficiently.

Partnership with parents

The 'Parent's Charter' makes it clear that parents have a right to be involved in their child's education, as well as a responsibility to support the school. It tries to raise the profile of the parent as 'customer' in line with other Charters, but the concept of the active and involved parent here is often not flexible enough for day-to-day practice. Many of the assumptions behind the Charter's approach betray a misunderstanding of the way some families function, especially those undergoing disruption and instability. There is always the danger that partnership is made available only on the school's terms – not a genuine meeting of equals at all but a discretionary opportunity offered only to those who can fit in with certain expectations.

'Home–school partnerships' have been promoted by many organizations including the National Association of Headteachers (NAHT), the National Confederation of Parent–Teacher Associations (NCPTA) and the Royal Society of Arts (RSA). These generally focus around commitments made in advance which set standards of good practice on both 'sides' and clarify mutual roles. But inevitably, such a model appeals most to the articulate, educated parent, whose own education was a generally positive experience. Many families will find this approach requires more guarantees than they can hope to deliver.

Most parents want their children to go to school (if only to get them out of the way!) but some feel distinctly ill-at-ease with teachers or find even coming on to school premises quite threatening. It is often difficult for school staff to appreciate this. I have worked with parents who live within sight of their children's school but who have never been able to walk through the gates. I suspect there is probably more 'school phobia' amongst parents than there is amongst children. If you do not feel articulate or able to compete with professionals (even if that sometimes comes out as aggression or indifference) or if your only contact with the school is when things go wrong, it can be very difficult to pick up and use the opportunities which schools must now make available.

Legislation requires schools to provide information for parents about their children's attendance and to publish statistical data in the annual report. Most schools will accept that such procedures do little to break down barriers and enable the reluctant parent to build a more creative relationship with them. Annual meetings are usually poorly supported and, when it comes to addressing issues such as attendance, the people you most want to be there rarely, if ever, turn up. It is easy to be cynical in this situation and to reinforce the stereotype that 'those sorts' of parents aren't interested, at the same time as the parents are probably moaning about 'that school' being snobbish and unwelcoming. The child's attendance is likely to slip down the hole in the middle of these prejudices.

A mutual obligation

It is obviously better to work with parents than against them wherever possible and such an approach is now underpinned by the philosophy of the Children Act 1989. It is parents who carry the final responsibility for their children, not schools. But the significance of this cuts both ways. It means that schools have every right to remind parents of their statutory duty for making sure that their children are properly educated. But it also means that professionals and agencies who work with other people's children should take care to involve the parents wherever humanly possible. It is their problem, but they cannot be expected to deal with it unless people tell them what's going on.

This is particularly important in 'split' family situations where a school would now be expected to make reasonable efforts to involve *all* those with 'parental responsibility' for the child, including any such person who lives apart from them, eg, a divorced father. 'Home–school liaison', vital though it is, does not necessarily cover all of the possibilities. Building effective relationships with parents may mean seeking creative and innovative ways of working together involving mum, dad, step-dad, grandma and the child – even if they won't all speak to each other!

The spirit of this dialogue should be consultation not condemnation. While it may be true that the parents are failing to discharge their duty, little progress is likely to be made if they feel that they have been contacted only so that they can be blamed. And such dialogue may have to happen in unconventional ways where parents do not, for example, respond to requests to visit the school or turn up for meetings.

Building trust
The requirements of the Education Acts 1944 and 1993 that schools should collect data about 'registered parents' for ballot purposes, and the need to know who has 'parental responsibility' under the Children Act 1989, have exposed a considerable lack of trust between some parents and their children's school. It can cause problems when parents are prepared to trust us with their child for 30 hours a week but do not trust us enough to supply much information about their family circumstances. This may still be seen as intrusive if there is no expectation of the relationship with school being very significant.

Schools will have to make sure that they know how to handle confidential information; parents are entitled to that reassurance. But we cannot work together if we are total strangers: if we do not even know with whom we ought to be partners! Breaking down barriers of ignorance and misunderstanding, on both sides, will be essential if we are to move towards working together to tackle absence. Involving parents will cost schools something; but the benefits are considerable.

Most problems between home and school come about as a result of failures of communication. There is no point in sending letters home and hoping for the best if experience has already shown that certain parents do not respond, especially if the letters contain only bad news or are couched in educational jargon. There is no substitute for personal contact and the establishment of pastoral relationships in which both parties can have some confidence. Too much contact between home and school is at the level of circular letters. Many parents do not read them, some cannot. Sometimes such circulars are unclear in their expectations or are not seen by the family as relevant to their particular circumstances.

One of the most depressing examples is the apparent growth of impersonal letters in response to poor attendance, informing parents that their child has been arbitrarily removed from the school roll. If there has been no response before, there is no point in adding yet more paper to the pile! Such unilateral action (without using proper exclusion procedures) probably has no legal basis anyway, but how is it intended to increase the parents' sense of partnership and responsibility?

In many families having difficulty getting children to attend school, the parents too are desperately concerned about the child's behaviour. They may be weary with the struggle or feeling guilty and powerless about their inability to resolve the problems. They already feel out of control of the situation. The last thing they need is further disempowerment by being treated in such a way. If parents do not come to school or answer letters because they have given up then something more creative is required, not more of the same but with added hostility.

Home visits by teachers
The issue of home visiting by teachers is contentious. In principle it would seem only common sense that going to where the child and parents are is a strategy well worth pursuing if they won't come to you. Many teachers would not, however, see this as part of their job and will prefer to use the EWO/ESW as a go-between or limit it to certain key individuals. Professional organizations of education social workers are usually concerned about it, and there are questions about insurance, but my experience has been that teachers have sometimes been helped immensely in understanding the child's difficulties by seeing them in their home environment. Where are they supposed to do the homework, or sleep? No wonder they're so often late when all *that* is happening every morning.

Some parents feel more confident when they are on home ground, though any such approach has to be with their consent. None of us, including an officer of the LEA, has the right to enter people's homes uninvited. ('Truancy officers' employed directly by schools, not the LEA, are in an especially vulnerable position and have *no* legal authority other than as an extension of the school's pastoral system.) In an ideal world I would ask all teachers to come back a few days earlier at the end of the summer holiday and spend the time calling on a few pupils to invite them back to school. I know it will never happen but in my opinion it would do wonders for bridge-building.

A welcoming environment

It is worthwhile making sure that the school is welcoming and accessible to parents. Again we may assume that it is, without actually checking. Are there proper facilities for seeing visitors or do conversations about children have to take place in noisy corridors and draughty corners? Who has the time to spend with parents as a clear part of their designated job, not as an unrecognized extra to be squeezed in between everything else? What about those who do not have their own transport or who have language or mobility difficulties? What impression is given when you first walk into the building or when you are trying to find your way from the car park?

Do people take the time in meetings to make sure that parents understand what is going on? Might some parents need advocates to speak on their behalf? Are they always expected to fit in with our timetables or are we prepared to see them outside their work time (which might otherwise cost them in lost wages)? It is no use expecting a parent who lives 100 miles away, but who still sees his or her child every other weekend and considers themself an active parent, to turn up on a one-off parents' evening like everyone else. They may need special arrangements and without them a resolution of the problem will not be found. How can people be kept informed if they can't be at meetings? Written records, letters or phone or follow-up visits, for example?

This will all be very time-consuming, but so is repeated failure. A great deal of time and energy may be expended on strategies which are never going to work for that particular parent or child. It should be a matter of policy that every effort is made to find a resolution by negotiation; through written agreements which set down what everyone, including the school, will do to improve things, or by accepting that unusual circumstances may require unusual solutions, like part-time attendance or education otherwise than at school. Our motive should always be twofold: the empowerment of parents, by helping them to accept responsibility for their child's education (with help), and the promotion of the child's welfare so that their best interests are served.

Rewards

It is much better to reward attendance than to punish absence. There tends to be a knee-jerk reaction amongst many people which leads to first thoughts being of how to *make* children and parents act responsibly rather than how to encourage them to do so and respond positively when they do. Headteachers and governing bodies should take the lead in establishing an atmosphere of positive incentive rather than relying too much on negative sanctions, many of which will in any case have little or no impact on those with the biggest problem. As poor attenders have so frequently pointed out to me, the teachers get paid for coming! Would they still do so if there was no pay-cheque at the end of the month?

This is not simply a trivial point. Most things in our society are valued in terms of their financial reward. Perhaps we should be thinking about whether children should be paid for coming, especially in the later years of compulsory education. They are paid for their part-time jobs as a reward for acting responsibly, like 'grown-ups in waiting'. Then, when it comes to school it's back to being treated like a child again; coming just because someone else says you must, even way past the age of 16 for some. The assumption that coming to school is of value purely in its own right will not cut much ice with many pupils. We are all interested in what we will get out in return for what we put in.

Building on strengths

School has all kinds of attractions and it is clearly very important as a way of making and maintaining peer group relationships. For many if not most pupils this will be just as significant a motivation as the lessons, no matter how much they enjoy individual subjects. It is one of the most helpful motives on which to work when children are frequently absent and one of the most severe consequences for those who develop persistent refusal. The fear of losing touch with friends can be a powerful incentive to return, until, that is, it becomes such an obstacle that it is easier to give up and stay at home.

This sense of the school day as a social occasion sometimes irritates teachers who feel that some children don't seem to realize that they have come to school to work. It can become a distraction and needs to be kept in perspective, but if we really want children to want to come, especially those who do not have high academic expectations, we ignore it at our peril. Opportunity during the day when children can spend time together relaxing is important – not only quality 'playtime' for the younger ones (with interesting and stimulating equipment, not just acres of bare tarmac), but also as space to explore relationships, gossip, compete, discuss TV and plan your life outside school – all vital social skills for any teenager. Providing places where such time can be spent, where young people feel that they can be themselves, is vital as a way of reinforcing the school experience.

Personal value
As with so much about the way education is sometimes managed, the needs of many children can easily be overlooked. This is made even more likely, of course, if they are not there very often. Some feel they have no stake in their school; no real voice in what goes on. The school is not really meant for children like them. Rewarding their positive contribution to its life will mean giving them real access to decision making and a sense that what they say is being heard. Adults in the workplace are not likely to show a very positive attitude if they feel that management takes no notice of them. Why should children be any different?

For the more able and motivated children, reward will come in the form of praise for good work, honours in sports or music, examination success and constant reinforcement from parents and teachers. Some children will know from the first that they will never be in this group, despite the very best endeavours of teachers to find other ways in which their attendance can be made worthwhile.

A school actively seeking to encourage attendance by these children will want to make sure that they feel rewarded and motivated by the knowledge that they are important within the school community; that they have a contribution to make, something to say worth hearing, that they are valuable for who they are, not just for what they can achieve. If there are only 'external' reward systems, exams, certificates, prizes and the like, some young people will not accept the basic rules of the game. They will not be impressed at the prospect of being clapped in assembly for good attendance; indeed the thought may horrify them. The ruler, pen or key-fob will do little to make them feel that it is worth coming in when they are tempted to stay in bed.

Such schemes have their place, primarily for the occasional truant who needs a reminder that failure may spoil an otherwise excellent record. But in my opinion they are of little value for the chronic refuser or the child who has lost all sense of the value of education. Class targets and incentive schemes will pass them by. They will actually be a liability to their peers and embarrassed about returning for fear of the flak they will receive for letting them down. For such children, those for whom much more is going on than normal teenage experimentation, it is much more important to send a signal that they are missed when they are not there and that they will be welcomed back.

Internal rewards
We have to stress the more *internal* factors like well-being, acceptance and 'unconditional positive regard' which will improve their feeling of self-worth. In a paper circulated at a truancy conference in late 1993, Mary Margaret Kelly argued that schools need to go much deeper than better surveillance by also trying to create an educational experience which is too attractive to be missed. Schools could act in a number of ways:

- empowering staff to deliver the curriculum in a differentiated manner, taking account of ability, learning styles and teaching styles;
- raising the profile of equal opportunities with a focus on race, gender, social circumstances and special educational needs;
- creating an ethos and climate in which pupils are able to grow as whole people with opportunities for moral and spiritual development;
- liaising effectively with parents and the community and making that liaison part of the learning process;
- providing a safe environment for pupils, with inbuilt procedures and strategies for dealing with personal or group problems;
- creating effective systems and practices for using the expertise of other professionals and the business community. (Kelly, 1993)

Whether or not you accept an overall counselling approach to truancy, it cannot be denied that the principles established in that field are relevant in any attempt to encourage better attendance. It would be foolish for schools to ignore the great wealth of experience amongst those who have also tried to facilitate behaviour change, especially by those who are perceived to have a problem:

> The client who is lacking in self-acceptance behaves in a way which reflects that attitude; he does not expect people to value him, so in relation to others he is self-protective or defensive. He may appear weak, inappropriately aggressive, unemotional, or perhaps he tends to withdraw from intense social contact.

Behaviours such as these are scarcely welcoming for other people, and may indeed drive them away, a fact which offers further evidence that the client is unloved and unlovable. Unconditional positive regard breaks into this cycle as the counsellor refuses to be deflected by the client's defensive behaviour and instead offers the client consistent acceptance of his intrinsic worth. (Mearns and Thorpe, 1992, pp.61–2)

For 'counsellor' read 'teacher' and for 'client' read 'child' and our schools would be transformed. We are so often deflected by the pupil's poor response, rapidly reaching the point where we feel we have nothing left but blame. Our reward systems are all based on achievement; they assume that a child will want to do what we want them to do in order to receive the reward which we are offering to them. By focusing on such external factors we will often fail to engage the child at all. Their lack of interest or even hostility will be misinterpreted and we will move on to other more 'deserving' cases, thereby compounding their sense of failure. No counsellor would make such a mistake because they are more concerned about the person within than whether or not they conform to our expectations.

Making time
It sounds rather pathetic but many poor attenders are desperate for someone to love them – unconditionally. Many of their parents will feel the same. Perhaps home is a place where you are only loved when you are good, or are hardly loved at all. Perhaps your experience of adults is that they are not to be trusted; they break their promises, put their own needs first, leave you and sometimes never come back. What a child most needs from school may be one person who will love them, not public praise but private empathy from someone who has the time and space to enter into their experience and to listen.

The worst thing we can do to a child is to make them feel as if they are of no value. Sadly the pressures on schools' pastoral care systems mean that there is often little opportunity to affirm them, especially if they do not give us much encouragement along the way! A colleague of mine once made an appointment to see a child at break-time. Two minutes into the conversation she stood up to go, not because she was bored but because she thought that was as much time as anyone ever had for you at school. She couldn't believe that he was prepared to spend the rest of the morning with her if necessary in order to talk through why she was being so disruptive on the rare occasions when she was there.

I make no apology for what might seem like an impossible expectation – that more children will come to school more regularly if someone will make time for them as a person; not minutes but hours if necessary. Our sense of care for the whole child used to be the strength of the British educational system. We did not regard children simply as learning machines come for a few hours programming. With the introduction of the market-place into schools this sense of a pastoral approach has been perhaps the biggest casualty, and the absence figures will be one sign of it. No one has time anymore: EWOs, parents, teachers are all too busy. If we really want to reward our pupils for coming, a positive commitment to making such resources available should be a priority.

It doesn't have to be a teacher. Teachers are not always very good at this; they're not usually trained for it and they have plenty of other things crying out for their attention. Some children will need skilled counselling. Volunteers might do a useful job – perhaps other parents with suitable guarantees about confidentiality. Some LEAs and schools have been experimenting with 'best friends' from the sixth form or recent school leavers to get alongside children with poor attendance and work with them one-to-one. They help with homework, take the kids on treats, act as a go-between between home and school, etc.

Headteachers and governors will want to ensure that a range of professional skills is available so that school becomes a place where children at risk feel understood; a place where you actually want to be because of all the positive reinforcement you receive there. All the new computerized registration equipment in the world will not encourage this kind of poor attender and sophisticated systems will have no impact on those who feel alienated and unwanted. It's down to priorities: how high up the scale do the needs of the absent come? However it is done, it should be a matter of clear school policy, not just left to chance. Otherwise children will simply vote with their feet.

REFERENCES

Carlen, P, Gleeson, D and Wardhaugh, J (1992) *Truancy – The Politics of Compulsory Schooling*, Buckingham: Open University Press.

DfE (1994) *School Attendance: Policy and practice on categorisation of absence*, London: DfE.

DES (1991) *The Education (Pupils' Attendance Records) Regulations, 1991, appendix 2*, London: DES.

HMI (1989) *Attendance at School – Education Observed No.13*, London: Her Majesty's Inspectorate.

Kelly, M M (1993) Handout at the 'Children on the Edge' conference, 17 November.

Mearns, D and Thorpe, B (1992) *Person-centred Counselling in Action*, London: Sage.

Reid, K (ed.) (1981) *Combating School Absenteeism*, Sevenoaks: Hodder and Stoughton.

5

Education Welfare
in the 1990s

THE STATUTORY SERVICE

A unique role

Barring a considerable change in legislation, it is anticipated that
local education authorities will be under a duty to monitor the
attendance of children at school for the foreseeable future, despite
the major changes in finance and management which are going on
elsewhere. The Education Act 1993 has restated previous provision
about the unique statutory function of the LEA. The government has
signalled its intention that from 1995 education welfare is to be
treated rather differently from most other LEA services, without the
same emphasis on competitive tendering within an open market.

Consequently, EWOs/ESWs are probably more secure than
almost any of their LEA colleagues, though some have seen
dramatic reductions in their funding and staffing levels in recent
years, just as public anxiety about truancy has increased! Such a
commitment from central government does not, of course, mean
that resources are always made available locally at the levels which
are required. There must be teachers too, but that doesn't remove all
possibility of shortages.

Any changes in future must recognize the relationship with
individual schools which is a hallmark of current services. Most
officers are based at local schools, operate a 'patch' system or have
built up an identity as part of a local educational support team. Few,
if any, within the service would welcome any restructuring which
would see them moved away from their school colleagues. However, many would also argue that too cosy a relationship threatens
the important impartiality which they have as representatives of
LEAs rather than as the agents of headteachers or governors.

There is undoubtedly pressure on EWOs/ESWs to see schools as their 'customers' and some greater element of accountability is reasonable. Our school-based colleagues have a right to ask what we are doing with resources which have not been made available for them to use themselves. But this may sometimes go too far if EWOs/ESWs are always expected to take the school's 'side' in any dispute. Some measure of independence is vital in order to ensure that vulnerable children are not lost in the system with no one to help them as they either pass from one school to another or do not attend for long periods.

The priority of attendance

Whatever happens, the government has clearly signalled its intention that the promotion of school attendance must be a central function of the service. The 1994 Guidance from the DfE on the categorization of absence repeats the statement first made in Circular 11/91 when the new registration regulations were introduced:

> The principal function of the education welfare service is to help parents and LEAs meet their statutory obligations on school attendance. The EWS is the attendance enforcement arm of most LEAs. Its officers are able to bring to the assistance of schools a wide range of skills. Through their home visiting, they may be especially well-placed to assess a non-attender's problems in the wider family context. Schools should develop an effective working relationship with Education Welfare Officers based on a clearly delineated division of labour. (DfE, 1994, para. 14)

This is interesting not least because it does *not* say that EWOs/ESWs should spend all their time helping schools to authorize their absences! If this is seen as the priority by headteachers, there will be little time left for the 'wide range of skills' or the 'wider family context'. The government is right to stress the need for clear decision-making about priorities and how the LEA's services can be best used. There will always need to be a balance between prevention and response; ideally one which has been worked out carefully at local school level.

A range of duties

Granted that attendance issues are the most important, it must first be acknowledged that there are many other functions which are also the statutory responsibility of the LEA. Many of them have been there for decades. This is not always recognized, especially given the pressure for a return to the language of 'attendance officers'. This work too is underpinned by legislation and it may be helpful to set out the wide range of duties which will currently fall on most EWOs/ESWs.

- Assessment of entitlement to free school meals, monitoring the review of claims, liaison with schools and benefit agencies (Education Act 1980). In my authority this amounts to the management of over 28,000 claims. This benefit is not, as many people assume, administered by the Department for Social Security, though it is restricted only to those claiming Income Support (ie, not Family Credit, Unemployment Benefit or any other benefit). Even with the introduction of computerized systems, this remains a major area of work and one which is still growing.

- Assessment of entitlement for other benefits such as clothing schemes, shoe funds and charitable grants. Practice here is more varied as these benefits are not an automatic entitlement and will be dependent on individual LEA provision. Some have delegated the budgets to schools, others have done away with such funds altogether. Many families struggling to cope on benefits or low incomes still turn to 'the welfare' for help and the EWO/ESW may be the only professional available to assist them with claims, appeals, etc. Most DSS offices will not give even loans for school clothing, let alone grants, though claimants may get limited help with shoes or coats provided they can repay the loan from their remaining benefit.

- Registration, monitoring and inspection of school-age children who are in part-time employment outside school hours (Children and Young Person's Act 1933, Education Act 1944 and local authority bye-laws). Many school staff, children, parents and employers do not realize that *all* such employment is illegal for a child under the minimum school-leaving age (not just under 16) unless the job is registered with the LEA. This is intended to protect children and to ensure that work does not interfere with school. Few LEAs give it very high priority, due to the pressure of other work, but there is still a real risk of children being exploited as cheap labour alongside the more traditional jobs like paper-rounds. The law is badly in need of modernization.

- Registration, monitoring and inspection of children who are taking part in entertainments (Children and Young Person's Act 1963 s.37 and the Children (Performances) Regulations 1968). Again many do not realize that legislation requires LEAs to license children for such activities and that this permission is required for the child to have any time off school. (Absences without such authority should not be authorized). While some of this provision dates back to a time when theatres were considered rather dangerous places for impressionable young minds (it still includes the appointment of 'matrons' and chaperones), there is an important need to safeguard against exploitation and to ensure that education is not adversely affected.

- Responsibilities under child protection procedures, as laid down by local Area Child Protection Committees (Children Act 1989 and the Department of Health inter-agency guide, 'Working Together'). It is vital that education is properly recognized as a crucial part of a child's life and that schools are aware of their role in the protection of children from abuse. While school staff face the day-to-day responsibility, EWOs/ESWs are essential contributors to case-conferences and the LEA has specific duties for inter-agency liaison, including during school holidays. Staff in schools cannot act without proper procedures, support and training and nearly all LEAs will see this as part of the role of their welfare service, in addition to the SSD.

- Responsibility for children with special educational needs, either as part of the statementing process by providing information about the child and family, or by acting as escort to children travelling to or from residential schools. This role has reduced in recent years as more children with special needs now stay in the local community, but it may still provide an essential link between home and school where long distances are involved and a useful arms-length role in ensuring that the needs of vulnerable children are being properly met. Escorting parents to enable them to participate fully in their child's education may also be important for those families unable to make their own travel arrangements.

- Many EWOs/ESWs have responsibilities towards excluded children. They may be involved in facilitating a change of school by advising parents, etc. or they may be a crucial part of LEA procedures for monitoring alternative provision such as home tuition or 'education otherwise'. With ever-larger numbers of children being permanently excluded from school, this is a growing area of work in many authorities.

- LEAs also have to be represented in inter-agency procedures for 'children in need' (Children Act 1989). The whole thrust of the Act is that agencies must work together and that, for example, assessments of need should be carried out by different agencies at the same time rather than by each in isolation. Children with special educational needs and excluded children will be covered by this concept, together with children whose families are undergoing serious disruption or disadvantage. LEAs have a statutory duty to cooperate in the provision of services for such children.

- There are similar procedures for children who commit offences where again there is a requirement that decision making is done on an inter-agency basis. This is usually through a Youth Liaison Panel on which the welfare service represents the LEA. School reports for Youth Courts may be required and, as with child protection and general services for children at risk, teachers need advice, training and support in carrying out these responsibilities.

- Some LEAs, though it is now a declining number, will expect their EWOs/ESWs to be involved in sorting out the free provision of transport to and from school. One of my first duties was walking a route to establish whether it was just under or just over three miles! Some officers however still have a major role in this area, especially in the distribution of bus passes in rural areas. There are also a variety of other odd functions like posting up public notices of proposed school closures or counting how many children cross authority boundaries to go to school.

Recent research

All this is in addition to duties relating to school attendance. And it still doesn't include the general role of 'children's friend', from urgent help for a distressed child through to the time when a young lad asked me what his friend should do if he fancied a girl in his class but was afraid to ask her out! Sometimes schools misuse their EWO/ESW, for collecting overdue library books or school photograph money, but there is a whole mass of indefinable work which will come the way of any officer who regularly calls into a school, from running a child up to casualty to bringing one back who has been found shoplifting at lunchtime. Hence the difficulty posed by any expectation that LEAs should place less emphasis on 'social work' and more on enforcement.

Other kinds of working relationships with families are also required and there will often be tensions between these roles, some of which are very much services, while others require the exercise of authority and a detailed knowledge of legislation. Only a few LEAs will have the resources to enable specialist staff to operate in different areas of expertise; most staff will have to play all these roles at once and will need considerable skill to do so effectively.

Evidence to support this wide-ranging role was provided by Peter Halford's (1991) research in 1991. Ninety-six per cent of LEAs responded to his survey and, while there was general agreement that school attendance took priority, there was much else besides. He draws three key conclusions. First, involvement in work other than attendance is increasing, largely under the pressure of new legislation such as the Children Act 1989.

Second, this range of work means that training is often inadequate for the roles to be carried out properly. While secondment to social work training courses was taking place in 40 per cent of the LEAs, it is also often the case that staff then go into other areas of social work and their expertise is lost. Very few courses recognize the particular specialisms of education social work.

Third, there are, as a consequence, questions about the status and professionalism of the service. The skills being demonstrated are far more wide-ranging than is usually recognized, with 97 per cent of Halford's respondents claiming that they offered 'counselling' to children and 90 per cent that they worked collaboratively with teachers and others. Officers may increasingly make use of group work or give specialist advice and training to schools and colleagues in other agencies. All of this suggests a need to recognize education welfare/social work as a valid profession with its own integral body of knowledge, rather than seeing it simply as knocking on doors and coercing children into school. This myth is still perpetuated, however, at both local and national levels, by both schools and other professionals. It clearly does not fit the reality, though local pay and conditions are often way below those of others with whom we work, as if the tasks were somehow less important and less skilled.

Areas of expertise
Southern (1992) has identified six functions carried out by education welfare officers, each of which is an expression of professional responsibility:

- linking home and school;
- helping people to obtain resources;
- influencing interactions between organizations;
- encouraging children to benefit fully from their education;
- influencing positive interaction between individuals;
- influencing school policy.

My own article in *Community Care* (Whitney, 1992), identified four areas of particular expertise.

- *School attendance:* rightly the first priority but undertaken within an increasingly inter-agency context, alongside professionals from other disciplines. EWOs/ESWs have developed considerable skills in problem-solving and the introduction of education supervision orders has required the acquisition of new skills in order to ensure their effectiveness. Careful assessment and realistic planning are essential in contexts where there may be no alternative solution other than a change in behaviour/attitude on all sides, always the most difficult of tasks.
- *Advocacy:* our clients are usually those with least access to resources, both in financial and in other terms (see, for example, Kumar, 1993). The inclusion of 'educational needs' as part of the 'welfare checklist' in the Children Act requires the promotion of children's welfare at school, even for those whose needs are difficult to meet or who may not seem to 'deserve' help. In an increasingly market-dominated environment in education, EWOs/ESWs will be amongst those seeking to protect the interests of children and parents who may bring their school little credit and who might be easily pushed aside for the sake of the majority.
- *Child protection:* not all school staff feel very confident in this area, despite their crucial role. Back-up services and providing year-round information are also required if the LEA is to discharge its duties appropriately.
- *Advice:* with the Children Act has come a massive change in perception of how schools should deal with separated, divorced and single parents. Most staff will need constant reassurance about the implications of 'parental responsibility' or the significance of new court orders, at least for the foreseeable future. Pastoral care is becoming increasingly complicated, against a background of a wide variety in family life and a quite proper emphasis on parents' rights to participate in their child's education, even if they are living apart from them. Much

current practice is having to change and staff whose primary qualification is that they know how to teach cannot be expected to deal with these issues without specialist support.

The 'Norwest' survey

All of which means that education welfare staff now seek to operate in ways which are often different from those which are expected. They are no longer content to be the 'general dogsbodies' which some would like, nor to be seen only as the enforcers of legislation, without concern for its effects on the individual problem. This is something of a contrast to the results of a survey of 'Norwest' by Carlen *et al.* (1992, ch.2) carried out in 1989, before the Children Act became law. This watershed is crucial and, for that reason, much of the research was already out of date by the time it was published. It provides more of a picture of practice as it was than practice as it is.

This research tended to confirm the rather negative and stereo-typed picture of EWOs and other professionals (crudely labelled 'truant-catchers' by the researchers) and the general ineffectiveness of their intervention. Unfortunately the researchers chose to concentrate on an extremely unrepresentative group of children with attendance problems, nearly 60 per cent of whom were also in the care of the local authority, many of them living in residential units after experiencing acute family breakdown.

Not surprisingly, work with this group achieved little improvement in school attendance and it is likely that workers in such situations were only too well aware of it. Little progress seems to have been made in resolving any of the issues in these children's lives. It is highly probable that suitable educational opportunity was not available; that is not the responsibility of those trying to help them. From this highly limited sample, the research paints a scenario of agencies 'targeting' certain families for court action through a variety of preconceived attitudes, with little thought to its effectiveness or justice.

A fair picture?

Most education social work practitioners would not accept that this represents a fair description of their work across the whole range of children who are having difficulty attending school, many of whom are not involved with other agencies at all. The children identified in this research were not primarily the responsibility of education welfare officers, nor was school attendance necessarily their major problem. The few stories of children facing less acute difficulty show a far higher degree of effectiveness, so not all the work is fruitless. But, most of all, EWOs/ESWs would now be very resistant to measuring our work by how many families are taken to court or how big the fines are.

We cannot avoid our legal duty altogether. Some children do need to know that there are boundaries to reasonable behaviour if they are to live in any kind of relationship with other people. We do them no favours by making no attempt to challenge them. There is still a need for some parents to be reminded of their responsibilities if they are compromising their child's right to education. Parents can behave selfishly and irresponsibly and no social work approach should simply overlook children's needs in order to avoid the difficult decisions.

But the research suggests an almost inexorable process, with increasingly punitive responses to continued absence from school almost as a matter of course. In fact, only a tiny minority of cases ever come to legal action and LEA procedures are designed to keep parents and children away from court wherever possible unless it is the best available way of resolving the problem. Statutory procedures now operating in Staffordshire, as set out below, enable a contrast to be drawn with those found by the researchers. I leave the reader to judge whether such a negative view of day-to-day practice is still appropriate.

GOOD PRACTICE IN EDUCATION SOCIAL WORK

Referrals from schools

Unlike most other social work professionals, EWOs/ESWs often have to work in a way which makes them responsible for vetting their own referrals. This is one of their most highly developed skills. A few services in urban areas are able to operate a formal referral and case-management system in which cases are allocated by a Team Manager according to the available resources of time, personnel, etc., but this system is not particularly popular, especially with schools.

The 'patch' system normally means that officers have to take everything that comes in their area, which, in some parts of the country, could include over 10,000 children in 25 or more schools. They will often have to seek out their own referrals by looking through registers or turning up at a school to see what the day brings. This has tended to make everything rather haphazard and can lead to wide variations in the quality of the information shared.

'Please will you find out what's happened to Mary Jones?' would not be the kind of referral accepted by a social services department, especially if it was scribbled on the back of an envelope or shouted down the corridor as the year head is about to disappear into assembly! I have known more than one occasion when my initial investigations centred upon the wrong child; there are often duplicates in school communities of 1,000 or more. Sometimes 'Mary Jones' is in school all along, or, more often, her mum has already rung in to explain that she's got tonsillitis but the message didn't get passed on. Good professional practice requires something rather more than this.

The role of the EWO/ESW
It is important to be clear about the role of the EWO/ESW; it is to:

- identify, in conjunction with schools, cases of non-attendance which necessitate further action;
- assess the circumstances which have led to the breakdown of attendance, identifying causes and other significant factors which may assist in resolving the problems;
- plan appropriate action in conjunction with the child, the family, the school (and involving any other specialist agency if necessary), in order to resolve the problems;
- implement such action plans to support the child and the family in overcoming their difficulties with school attendance;
- evaluate, in partnership with the school, the outcome of such action plans;
- maintain a record of the work undertaken;
- initiate court action, if appropriate, on behalf of the LEA. (Staffordshire LEA, 1994)

Quality referrals
None of this is possible unless proper arrangements are in place for the sharing of information. In primary schools this might be arranged when required; in secondary schools there should be timetabled meetings to which both sides give priority and in which the task can be addressed in a professional way. Referrals should be in writing and contain all the information needed for a proper response to be made:

- the child's full name, date of birth, address and year group/class;
- details of their family situation, names of parents and whereabouts of all those with 'parental responsibility' under the

Children Act 1989, including those who live apart from the child, and whether there are any court orders in force;
- statistical information relating to the child's absence and attendance during the period prior to referral; whether or not the absences have been authorized and, if so, on what grounds;
- any information which the school has relating to the possible causes of the absence, including contact with parents and what the school has already done to resolve the issues;
- the member of staff responsible for the referral and when they are available to discuss it in person;
- opportunity for the EWO/ESW to respond and an indication of the urgency involved.

Getting all this information *before* contacting the family will reduce the risk of unwarranted intrusion or wasting everyone's time. Now that most schools are using computerized systems for storing parent and pupil data and growing numbers are using computerized registers, there should be less reason than ever for inadequate data on which to work. Of course there may be gaps in information, though this may be because the correct questions have not been asked before. Gaps which are left consciously can be managed; gaps which are left because no one thought to find out first can lead to misunderstanding and confusion.

It is essential that staff appreciate that promoting attendance and combating absence is *everyone's* responsibility, not merely something to be pigeon-holed for the EWO/ESW when they are next in the building. Attendance problems are rarely life-and-death issues and there is usually time for consultation and preparation if it is not clear whether referral is appropriate. It is odd that some schools published extremely low rates of 'unauthorized absence', yet they made frequent referrals to their EWO/ESW! Many of these might have been for reasons other than attendance of course, so it is helpful for any referral form to provide an opportunity for concern to be expressed about other issues such as behaviour, substance misuse or family problems. Particularly in high schools, such procedures should be a matter of policy, agreed by the governors, monitored by them and about which they receive regular reports from both teaching staff and the EWO/ESW.

Using written agreements

One of the major impacts of the Children Act 1989 on all social workers has been the move to working by agreement with parents and children wherever possible. Court procedures are not needed if the parties are willing to work cooperatively together. Children may be 'accommodated' by the local authority as a service where a care order would not be appropriate. Orders will be avoided in private law issues such as divorce unless they are needed for the resolution of some dispute. Everyone has a right to know what is going on, to see all the papers and read all the reports. Decisions should include all those who are affected by what is happening, including the child where they are old enough to understand what is involved.

This philosophy should be more true in education than anywhere else. 'Parents' have a wide range of rights with respect to their children's education and should always be given opportunity to participate. Despite the UK's ratification of the United Nations' Convention on the Rights of the Child in 1991 however, the idea that children themselves should be consulted and involved often comes as something of a surprise, both to them and to some professionals. We are often wrestling with a tension between good social work practice and the inevitably hierarchical structures of authority which operate in many schools and families.

Clarifying expectations
Some children may try to abuse the idea that they will be treated more equally in decision making or may find it difficult to switch from being the rather passive recipients of education one minute to an active participant with a right to be heard the next. Sometimes it seems to them that no one else is being asked to change, only them. Some teachers find the change of role towards more equal negotiation difficult and even threatening. Parents often feel that they are expected to carry sole responsibility, when they feel there is more that others could be doing to resolve the situation.

Issues such as these are best addressed by the use of written agreements. These are not the same as 'contracts' which set down only what the child or parent must do and which many families see as simply setting them up to fail. Contracts which require the child to make all the promises can lead to resentment and feelings of injustice which may seem quite unreasonable to those who hold all the cards but which render progress impossible. Agreements, by contrast, ask for commitment on *all* sides towards an achievable objective and they will aim to offer a way forward on the basis of give-and-take which is ultimately in everyone's interests.

Such agreements sometimes operate informally: 'You stay away and I won't do anything to chase you up' or, 'Provided you tell us he's not fit for school, we'll accept your word for it and authorize the absence'. There is a great temptation, especially with Y11 pupils who have little to look forward to, to devise an agreement in which everyone feels they have won: the child doesn't have to come in anymore; the parent can avoid the daily aggravation; the school can improve its figures and the EWO/ESW can think about someone else for a change! I would never want to lose the flexibility which sometimes means that a nod and a wink is the best for everyone. Creating extra opportunities for extended work experience, even if they are not strictly legal, is one common example.

But such a system can operate against the best interests of children, where all the power is held by schools and professionals. It is often better to write the agreement down, not because this gives it any force whatsoever as a legal document, but because it may clarify boundaries, help parents to take more responsibility and lower the risk of misunderstandings. It gives a context against which to judge progress so that the effectiveness of the intervention can be measured relative to other approaches. It may help the child or parent to see that other people are genuinely trying to help them or provide a means of concentrating more effectively on the problem in hand in the clear knowledge of what the consequences of success or failure would be.

Quality agreements
Agencies which make more use of agreements have enabled us to learn from their experience in identifying what constitutes good practice. The best agreements:

- are written down and copied to everyone involved;
- are the product of negotiation/include the wishes of all participants, not simply one view imposed on others;
- don't commit anyone who is not a party to the agreement;
- should give a clear indication of goals, (including any dispute about what they are);
- should be accessible (language, style, etc.);
- stick to the point;
- offer short-term, achievable objectives;
- offer give-and-take on all sides;
- don't promise what cannot be delivered;
- state the consequences of success and failure;
- include arrangements for review;
- set out what parties can do if they feel aggrieved.

Agreements are useful, even if they do not work, for example for clarifying the circumstances under which absences will be authorized or left unauthorized. If they fail because of action or inaction by parent or child, then at least there can be some acceptance that agencies and schools have tried their best and they provide clear evidence that voluntary attempts at resolution have been exhausted. If the failure is beyond the family's control, such as the non-availability of some resource, or if parents have done everything which was asked of them, agreements help to avoid the injustice of their having to answer to a court for what is not their fault.

Inter-agency consultation

If initial investigation and response have not resolved the problem, and written agreements are not succeeding, the next step must be to consult with any other persons who may have a role to play in moving things forward. Some of these will be other educational professionals, like special needs coordinators or educational psychologists, if this hasn't happened already. This is especially important now that the Education Act 1993 places a clear duty on schools and LEAs to make provision for children with emotional and behavioural disorders (of which levels of attendance may be a specific indicator). Absence from school should not be an obstacle to special educational provision; it may be part of the evidence that alternatives are required.

It may be necessary to ask for assessments from other agencies, either social services or child health services, especially where the source of the problems is held to be outside the school. No LEA should now be proceeding to court action in the face of failure to resolve things by agreement, unless they are satisfied that no other avenue is more appropriate or yet to be explored. A great deal has to be done prior to such a decision, and schools must expect to make an active contribution alongside other professionals. Formal consultation with the SSD is a legal requirement before consideration can be given to an education supervision order; it is good practice in all cases where wider family issues are significant.

It is usually best if the education welfare service is responsible for this liaison rather than the school. Senior staff may chair a formal case-conference or convene some kind of inter-agency group to meet the child, parents, school and anyone else with a particular interest. Understandably, school staff often find it difficult to make time for such meetings, but in my view they are essential. They act as 'gate-keeping' for statutory action but, far more often, by bringing everyone together, they enable some other resolution to be achieved in the light of all the facts.

Some parents and children do not face up to the issues until confronted by such a forum. They are often surprised by the scale of the problem or to find that people are still willing to help them, and begin to open up to a more trusting relationship. These meetings are not the same as being summoned to the school or education office for a 'dressing down'. Such an approach merely alienates those whose behaviour we are trying to change and is largely counter-productive. Meetings should provide a place where everyone will be listened to and, even if the ultimate decision is that it is best for the child that the parents be prosecuted, ensure that parents and pupils are treated with the respect to which they are entitled.

Consultation procedures

Such opportunities for consultation should be a balance of formality and informality. Agencies which have something to say should be prepared to write down their concerns in advance, produce appropriate evidence to justify their claims and ensure that such reports are shared with parents and children prior to the meeting. Clear records of attendance patterns, behaviour and achievement should be provided, not just vague generalizations. Decisions should be recorded in writing and circulated to all those involved, including the child wherever appropriate.

Sometimes such inter-agency discussion produces only the negative 'cycle of blame' to which Carlen *et al.* (1992) refer (see Chapter 4). There is still too much buck-passing, especially when it comes to uncooperative young people. There might even be conflict over whether or not going to school is so important. School staff in particular will find this very frustrating where other colleagues do not necessarily share their perspective. But, painful though this process may be, it is preferable to putting the child's welfare further at risk by avoiding the difficult decisions, acting in isolation or seeking only a cosmetic solution.

LEAs do not carry the major responsibility for helping children and families in trouble. If the problem is not basically about school then it is wrong to make education the focus simply because that may seem the easiest law to enforce or because that's where the child is showing his or her hurt. It is here that I hope that Carlen's researchers would notice a significant change; one which has moved away from statutory action for its own sake, simply because there is nothing else left to do, and on to an approach which digs deeper into what is going on and then tries to assess who might be best placed to do something about it: child, parent, school, SSD, EWO/ESW, health professional, etc.

Using the courts

Not all problems are resolved by negotiation. A small minority will require action through the courts, provided there is some realistic hope that this action will prove beneficial and there is evidence on which to proceed. School staff sometimes expect EWOs/ESWs to get to this point more quickly, and there are times when postponing the inevitable is not in the child's best interests. Some officers are nervous about court or are not adequately trained and resourced to make sufficient use of the powers which are available. But using legal powers is a serious matter and should never be the preferred option while any other remains unexplored.

Even court procedures can be carried out in a way which keeps open the possibility of resolution by other means. This is often effective; indeed my experience would tend to be that if the procedure does not change things along the way, the eventual outcome in court may well also be unsuccessful. Even if parents are being prosecuted there are still ways of making sure they are aware of their rights, kept fully informed of what is going on and given every opportunity to suggest alternative solutions. Where children are the focus, LEAs should be making sure that they are properly represented and that attention is paid to enabling their voice to be heard. They are not on trial and this should be made clear to them.

Using the courts is a skilled professional task, especially in the Family Proceedings Court (where any appeals are to the High Court). EWOs/ESWs require access to proper legal advice and representation on the same basis as social workers from the SSD. Thankfully, the practice of being both prosecutor and chief witness seems to be dying out, giving both parents and officers a fairer deal. It is quite unreasonable to expect staff to play both roles – and then to carry on working with the family afterwards to ensure that some positive benefit comes from the proceedings! No court action removes the responsibility for the child's education from the parent altogether. Even here practice should be about empowerment if there is to be any hope of improvement.

Facing up to failure

When all agencies have been given the opportunity to act, or all statutory powers have been either used or rejected as inappropriate, no resolution may be possible. Often the correct educational provision is not available. We do not have all the answers to society's ills. It is difficult to accept defeat and I am particularly worried by the families in which children are in total control of what happens so that no one is able to exercise any influence over them. This is not the same as giving children a voice and treating them with respect, and it can render any kind of progress impossible.

Doing nothing in situations like these may be seen, especially by teachers, as allowing the child or parent to 'get away with it', though a longing for some kind of punishment has to be measured against the probability that it too will bring about little progress. There is, after all, likely to be a heavy price paid by the child in terms of lost development or disadvantage in employment, if not sooner then later, even if no one seems too worried about this at the time. All the evidence is that pushing parents and children further up the tariff in the past, leading ultimately to heavy fines or care proceedings, only made bad situations worse. Some situations are probably best left alone.

I often find myself working with families who have gone through all of the old responses before with younger children and they're still here; still unconvinced about the value of education, still struggling to cope with problems previous intervention has left entirely unresolved. There is little to be done at this late stage. Ultimately children grow up and it is remarkable how many of them seem to emerge from the cocoon of adolescence as really quite nice people, despite our very best endeavours!

Partnership

All of this process is about partnership: a much over-used word but there really is no other. Education social work starts from the principle that it is only by working together that we will resolve problems. Almost by definition, once we have sunk into conflict we have failed, and no amount of threatening will make much difference. People do not become more positive about education for fear of the consequences if they don't.

Only a tiny minority of children or parents are deliberately being anti-social, and even if they are, there is often a reason behind their hostility. Most families struggling with poor attendance are simply in a hole. Even if it is one of their own making, which it rarely is alone, our task is not to heap further dirt on top of them but to offer them a hand in climbing out. It is always very sad when they choose not to trust us, but we do not make them more likely to do so by taking away the ladder as a punishment!

STORIES

The following brief case-histories are based on examples from my own caseload. The names used are fictitious and they are not necessarily accurate in every detail so as to avoid any direct identification. They are intended to illustrate a range of responses to issues of poor attendance, especially those where resolution is not immediately obvious by conventional means. I hope they provide examples of the good practice outlined above. They are not all success stories – that would give an unfair picture of what the work is like. Neither are most 'truants' like this. Perhaps these examples demonstrate in particular the need for specialist social workers within education and that, especially where problems are greatest, only the formation of flexible working relationships gives any real hope of improvement. If teachers, parents, children and agencies cannot find an answer, there is often little the law can do to make it more likely.

Hannah (Y9/10)

Hannah only began to miss school towards the end of Y9. The school had very little contact with her parents and information was very sketchy. There was no dispute that the absences were mostly unauthorized. After much effort to break through their embarrassment, her mum and dad confided to the EWO that they were finding it difficult to limit her relationship with an older boyfriend and they felt they were losing control of her. This greatly worried them and there were many arguments within the family, especially about school. Hannah then took an overdose and rumours began to circulate at school that she had had an abortion. Specialist agencies offered help and support to the family, but everyone agreed that care proceedings wouldn't be appropriate. Eventually Hannah asked to change school and make a new start, though this was only partially successful. Her parents continued to try to meet her half-way as she was adamant she would not end the relationship and they did not want to risk her leaving home and being at even greater risk. Clearly prosecution would do little to encourage them. A new EWO is trying to win Hannah's confidence, but it continues to be touch and go whether she will attend school often enough to get anywhere near achieving her full academic potential.

Marie (Y7) and Darren (Y9)

Marie and Darren have lived with their father since his marriage ended some years ago. Both have been having frequent absences, usually at the same time. During the last year, their father has been diagnosed as having cancer and is in generally poor health. Sometimes he writes notes to cover their absences giving reasons such as shopping, hospital appointments or minor illnesses. Most of these have been authorized by the school. Involvement by the EWO has brought about little improvement as both children admit to considerable anxiety about leaving their father. Marie in particular says she is often afraid he will die while she is at school. The EWO and a social worker from the SSD work together in planning support services involving a Family Aide and some volunteers. It takes a long time for the children's dad to understand that he needs to think about their future, not just his own, as he is often depressed by his condition. Eventually an agreement is drawn up involving a community care package, regular phone calls home from school, new home–school contacts on a regular basis and specialist counselling for Marie. An education supervision order might be useful if the agreement fails, but prosecution is wholly inappropriate.

Joanne (Y10/11)

Joanne's attendance has been poor since she started her GCSE courses. When in school she is generally uncommunicative and uninterested. She has few friends and school staff cannot recall ever meeting her parents. Visits by the EWO reveal she lives with her mum, but there is rarely anyone at home. Cards left are not returned and two meetings have been cancelled at the last minute when her mum rang to say she was ill. By visiting during the evening some contact is at last established. Joanne's mum admits that she lets her spend time with her older sister nearby while she is at work. An agreement is drawn up setting out tighter procedures about whether absences will be authorized, with extra help in school to help Joanne catch up missed work. Joanne continues to be very withdrawn and unresponsive to the EWO's attempts to build a closer relationship with her. The agreement works for a while, but more formal meetings are needed when things break down and Joanne's mum again does not keep to the agreed procedures for verifying her absences. By now Joanne is just into Y11 but has missed a great deal. The LEA prosecutes her mother and, after an adjournment during which there is still no progress, she is fined. Joanne continues to be absent and is not entered for any GCSEs.

Robert (Y7/8)

Robert, together with his older brother Grant (Y11), have never been good attenders. They rarely attend for more than 50 per cent of the time. The EWO is a regular visitor to the home, where there is always a crisis of some kind going on: changing relationships, threats of eviction, minor illnesses, lack of money. Robert is able to exploit this situation and things usually pick up after a bit of encouragement, but he has made a particularly poor start to his secondary career. There has never been any question of major threats to Robert's welfare and the SSD is not involved. After many failed attempts to reach lasting arrangements, it is agreed to apply for an education supervision order. Robert's parents support the application as they accept they need help, though Robert initially instructed his solicitor to oppose it. The order is made however, and a new EWO is allocated to be the supervisor. On the whole, the more structured relationship works well. Robert takes to his new adviser and two members of staff at school are given a special responsibility to befriend him. Robert does well to get his attendance up to about 80 per cent. The real test will come when the order ends.

Carl (Y6)

Carl has been refusing to go to school since the beginning of his last year at primary school. He is reluctant even to get out of bed and his parents have sometimes been reduced to carrying him screaming to the car. However, he then refuses to get out when they arrive at school or threatens to run away. On the advice of the EWO his parents ask their GP to refer the family to a Child and Family Service. They recommend a programme of behaviour modification: establishing boundaries, being firm, using rewards, etc. In general, this makes little difference. Carl sometimes refuses to go with them to the clinic or comes but will not join in. The involvement of an educational psychologist proves more productive, though it took a long time to organize. In the meantime his parents were offered a home tutor by the LEA for a few hours a week. The psychologist devised a reintegration package, gradually introducing Carl to time at school; first when it is closed, then just for half an hour, etc. No one has been able to explain why he has reacted to school in this way as once he is there he shows no signs of distress and can easily manage the work. It seems Carl will always need a lot of help and it is unclear what will happen on secondary transfer. No law has been broken throughout as the school has authorized all his absences on medical grounds.

Liam (Y9/10)

Liam first came to the EWO's attention after two short-term exclusions for fighting. Home visits uncovered the story of major problems. His mum had recently moved out to live at the other end of the country and his dad was struggling to cope with Liam, his younger sister and his job.

He had been threatening to have Liam 'put away' and there had been considerable violence between them during frequent arguments. After his second exclusion Liam stopped going to school altogether. He often didn't keep appointments with the EWO and then suddenly moved to live with his mother. This only lasted a few months; he came back to his dad during the summer holiday, having left after a fight with his mum's new partner, sleeping rough in London on the way. Liam still didn't go to school and increasingly became beyond his father's control. After referral to the SSD, it was agreed that he be 'accommodated' in a local residential unit, with education provided through a part-time tutor. This worked quite well and he began to do some study for the first time in almost a year. However, he suddenly left the unit with his mother after a Saturday visit and went back to live with her. On checking the situation a few weeks later he had moved on again, probably back to London.

Kelly (Y10/11)

Kelly has never been a very good attender, but managed to keep her head above water until her GCSE years. She then fell seriously behind with long absences, explained by her mother as 'family problems'. When she did come in, she was often late and didn't sign in. There had been a great deal of conflict between Kelly and her younger sister and, for a while, she moved in with a neighbour under the supervision of the SSD. However, there has been some improvement in family relationships and she is back home again, still turning up at school only for odd days. Kelly says school is boring and she can't see the point of it. She stays up very late at night, and so gets up very late in the morning, but she is not generally beyond control or at risk of 'significant harm'. After various failed agreements and endless meetings, the LEA obtains an education supervision order – more in hope than expectation! Her mum values the support and Kelly is always friendly, though she rarely takes much notice of the advice or 'directions' she is given. She still stays away from school most of the time but, at a review, the supervisor suggests she do some courses at the local FE college. Kelly is scarcely enthusiastic, but she does put in a reasonable effort and is working on a couple of GCSEs. This might have happened without the order, but at least it has helped to establish some boundaries.

REFERENCES

Carlen, P, Gleeson, D and Wardhaugh, J (1992) *Truancy – The Politics of Compulsory Schooling*, Buckingham: Open University Press.

DfE (1994) *School Attendance: Policy and practice on categorisation of absence,* London: DfE.

Halford, P (1991) unpublished M. Phil. submission.

Kumar, V (1993) *Poverty and Inequality in the UK: The effects on children,* London: National Children's Bureau.

Staffordshire LEA (1994) *Attendance and Absence,* draft guidance to schools.

Southern, I (1992) 'Whither the Education Welfare Service?', *Journal of Education Social Work,* 1, Autumn, p.8 ff.

Whitney, B (1992) 'A time to Act', *Community Care,* 4, 6, pp.22–3.

6

Forward to the Past?

TRUANCY REDISCOVERED

A performance indicator?

It is often said that truancy is now on the nation's agenda as never before, though it could be argued that it has been there all along and that only the profile is new. Each new generation appears to have rediscovered the issue; none has yet been able to resolve it. I suspect that much of the present concern is related to the general climate of debate about family values and to the particular personality and background of John Patten, as much as to strictly educational issues.

Clearly the government has an interest in making sure that its wide-ranging reforms of recent years are a success. There is still anxiety about the educational standards shown by many of those leaving school, with less than half achieving satisfactory results in a range of core subjects. Children whose attendance is poor are rightly seen as not giving themselves sufficient chance to meet their full potential and under-achievement represents a tragedy not only for them as individuals but for society as a whole.

There has been such upheaval since the 1980s, not only in terms of school management and finance, but also involving the curriculum, testing and performance tables, that the recognition of some problems as still unresolved represents a major challenge for the future. What is the point of reform if children are not there to benefit? Shouldn't an improved commitment from pupils and parents be one of the signs that the reforms are working? 'Truancy' tables are intended to be a performance indicator, not just of pupils and parents but of schools. If they were actually used as a way of recognizing the criticisms children have of what is on offer, I for one would give them a greater welcome.

The Truth about Truancy

Crime prevention

But the debate is also about much wider questions because the link is constantly being made between truancy and crime, one of the government's main concerns and on which much of its credibility rests. Despite the fact that research continues not to establish a direct link between the two (including even the DfE-sponsored study by the University of North London Truancy Unit), Mr Patten's influence has encouraged everyone to see tackling truancy as part of a concern brought with him to the DfE from the Home Office.

Much of the enthusiasm for 'Truancy Watch' schemes and the more active involvement of the police comes from a desire to reduce crime as much as to increase school attendance; indeed, at times, it is clearly the more important objective. (This, not party political considerations, is why some LEAs are less than enthusiastic about the idea.) Only a few of those children who are absent from school commit offences, and many of those who present the biggest offending problem will probably be permanently excluded or awaiting admission to some scarce resource rather than 'playing truant'. Deterring the crime will not, in itself, ensure that their educational prospects are improved.

But the abduction and murder of Jamie Bulger in 1993 by two young boys who were absent from school seems to have had an incalculable effect on public perceptions. It has increased the likelihood of truants being seen as at least potential criminals, even if they are not there already. Statistics on crime reduction are given just as much prominence in assessing the value of street patrols, etc. as is any evidence of increased school attendance (often much more difficult to demonstrate as a direct consequence of this approach).

In my opinion, much of this response serves to deflect us from the real issues about why children are choosing not to go to school. The Bulger case, distressing and tragic though it was, is such a one-off that no serious conclusions about school attendance can be drawn from it. Surely it might equally have happened on a Saturday afternoon or during a holiday? I suspect that the whole incident tells us more about adults than it does about children.

Of course it is a good thing if shoplifting and car crime can be reduced, but do such things never happen outside school hours? It is right to take a pastoral interest in whether children should be at school, but simply moving them from one place to another, even frog-marching them to school and then watching them run out the back door, does nothing to tackle what is really going on. Confusion

110

of purpose may mean that we deal with neither truancy nor juvenile crime effectively.

Defining priorities

In the face of such uncertainties, there is a wide-ranging discussion going on about how to deal with those who do not attend school properly, in which the views expressed, even by those who agree about other things, can be extraordinarily diverse. Even those of us who are most involved are uncertain about the way forward. It is depressing when children constantly let you down or seem determined to go ever further down the road towards self-destruction. At times it is tempting to lapse into despair or anger, whether or not it improves the situation. But the decisions which we make at this point, and over the next few years, about which direction to go in, must be rational and considered, not based only on a desire to make ourselves feel better. We actually have to tackle the problems, not simply thrash about hoping for the best.

I suspect that ESWs/EWOs and schools will be asked to go in different directions at the same time, despite the rhetoric and tabloid headlines which reduce the issues to simplistic solutions. Human behaviour is always much more complicated than our systems will allow. There is no certainty that one particular approach will always work. But the outcome of the debate might well influence which initiatives receive the publicity and the resources, even if they are ineffective, and which will go on unnoticed, even if they prove moderately successful.

There is often such a difference between perception and reality. When the 1994–5 Grants for Education, Support and Training were announced, totalling £14 million of extra money for LEAs to tackle truancy, few, if any, noticed that only £500,000 was earmarked for high-profile projects such as patrols in shopping centres, etc. The rest was for a variety of projects, from electronic registration systems through to specialist school-based support staff, training programmes and extra EWOs/ESWs to work directly with children and families. Some well-proven schemes lost their funding altogether and staff lost their jobs. All this, however, went unreported; media interest focused entirely around the images of police officers on patrol – for a day or two!

This tends to lead to a similar emphasis amongst local politicians and headteachers. Suddenly everyone wants to *see* 'something' being done about truancy. Profile is everything. The image of the EWO/ESW patiently negotiating a way out of conflict or sitting for two hours while a child gradually unloads their burdens of anger and disappointment attracts no one – even when it succeeds. While there is always a temptation to take the money and run, the perspective of education social work counsels caution if anyone imagines that long-term solutions can be found by short-term gimmicks. If the answers were that simple, everyone would have done it long ago. Many have already tried and moved on to something else.

FUTURE TRENDS

There are a number of ways of characterizing possible trends for the future, but I have chosen to set them out as a series of tensions. These are not necessarily mutually exclusive, but they illustrate the extremes of each continuum, even if resolution is often found somewhere in the middle. Different agencies in society may take up different stances with respect to the same child and family; much inter-agency work founders on the rocks of mutually incompatible expectations. There is no consensus, but in my judgement each of the following areas will require attention, even though change could come from any of a number of different directions.

Punishment v. welfare

This is the most obvious area of dispute as society wrestles with how to deal with young people who choose not to conform with the majority expectation. Clearly school attendance issues do not operate in a vacuum when it comes to the nation's moral sentiments and much of our thinking is inconsistent. It is possible to have an outcry about 'pindown' one moment (when it was judged indefensible for children to be kept confined or in their pyjamas in a residential care unit), and the introduction of 'secure training orders' the next (when children as young as 12 may be sent to secure establishments based on rigorous discipline).

Similar inconsistencies apply over child protection issues. There is considerable support (even within the government) for physical punishments to be reintroduced into schools, alongside widespread condemnation of the physical abuse of children, with statutory procedures designed to prevent it. Smacking is said to be harmless, but examples constantly tell us that what begins as 'appropriate' can degenerate into assault when misused.

The prevailing mood may frequently change. There is often more interest in retribution than in actually making sure that people change as a result of what we do. We are damned if we act and damned if we don't; over-intrusive one minute, guilty of failure to intervene the next. Social work as a solution to society's ills has never had a good press but, when they have a problem, people still want it done by someone. Those of us who wish to advocate a more compassionate response to children's problems probably face an uphill task in the next few years, despite the Children Act which, typically, is already being quietly forgotten in some quarters.

Changing the law?

For more punitive ideas to take hold about absence from school, a number of legal changes would be necessary. Parents could be held more accountable for their children's behaviour (as has happened in changes to the criminal justice system), even where they themselves have done everything reasonably possible to ensure that their children attend. No doubt some would argue that this power already exists and that LEAs should prosecute parents more readily.

Certainly the implication of such an approach would be to abandon all ideas of partnership. Parents will not turn to us for help if they think that they will end up in court as a result. Unless they have clearly failed to act responsibly in some way, such a response risks rewarding the child for their behaviour by making life more difficult for their parents – precisely what the child is often trying to achieve where family relationships have broken down.

In any case, there is little that can be done to punish parents more severely for their children's failure to attend school. Maximum fines against parents have recently been raised to £1,000, though magistrates rarely treat the cases brought before them with such severity and have to take ability to pay into account. Imprisonment as a possible sanction was only removed with the Children Act so it is difficult to conceive of any greater sanction against parents other than higher fines, even though many would not be able to pay them without the family breaking up and the children's welfare being put at risk as a result. Granted that our prisons are already full to overflowing with non-payers and our child care resources stretched to the limits, it seems unlikely that anyone will seriously advocate a return to previous provision here.

Targeting children

However, increasingly repressive measures against children may be more popular. One of the most probable suggestions is that children of age 10 and over who are caught committing offences when they should be at school might be made subject by the Youth Court to some kind of supervision over school attendance as part of the sentence imposed for their crime. Failure to attend regularly might result in them being brought back before the court again. More serious, even custodial, penalties could then be imposed for the original offence because they have failed to keep to the required conditions, even if they have committed no further offences in the meantime.

Two points about this possibility need to be made clearly. First, this could only relate to those who commit criminal offences *as well as* not going to school. This will involve only very few children and will have no impact at all on the vast majority of absentees who are entirely law-abiding. Many of those who offend will be out of the local school system anyway and enforcing their attendance may therefore be impossible.

Second, this would not be the same as placing a child on an education supervision order under the Children Act, though perhaps this approach might fall into relative disuse if the climate (and the resources) favour other approaches. ESOs give the supervisor from the LEA no power to bring the child back before the court for punitive sanctions if the order fails; they are 'welfare'-based in line with all proceedings under the Act, made by courts which do not deal with criminal matters. They are more about protection than punishment. Children cannot 'breach' an ESO and no other outcome can be imposed as a result of failure unless the social services department takes the view that care proceedings are needed, which will be very rare.

The limits of force

Some press reports have again suggested that EWOs/ESWs might be given powers to 'arrest' young people who are not in school and return them by force. Any such suggestion betrays a dangerous lack of awareness of the problem. Unless truancy itself is an offence, what right would anyone have to detain a child against their will? The police already have the necessary powers under the Children Act if the child is suffering or at risk of 'significant harm' and needs protection. What will happen when children and young people resist or allege assault against the officer trying to detain them? Will employers be willing to pay for all the extra sick leave caused by the stress and injury that would result from such pointless confrontations?

Indeed, the difficulty with any attempt to force children to go to school (and stay there) is the impossibility of making it work. Anyone advancing such a notion has never stood outside a child's bedroom door (locked on the inside) trying to persuade them to get dressed and come to school with you. Even where parents are quite prepared for you to break the door down and carry the child into school against their will, no one should now be willing to do it and no school could be expected to hold on to them. It is simply not practicable, let alone the human rights issues involved.

The truth is that no one can force a child into school. Threats tend to make things worse, not better. Even a specialist unit for school refusers cannot be a prison and a local comprehensive certainly never can be. Violence, caning and the like, will do nothing to improve the situation. Punishing children further, when they are already hurting themselves more than anyone else by their action, is a nonsense.

Reinventing care?
There might also be a move to reinstate the idea that children should go into local authority care if they do not go to school. This has proved to be unproductive in the past and would prove equally so in the future unless children are to be confined to secure units and receive their education there. Social workers will be very reluctant to be seen as agents of control for children who do not attend and massive changes in legislation would be required. Residential provision is being closed down all over the place as not being in children's best interests and I cannot imagine that SSDs would welcome its return. It is possible, I suppose, that some private agency might be invited to tender for new 'approved schools' for truants but the Department of Health would be highly unlikely to support such an initiative.

The only alternative to 'welfare' is to lock more children up and perhaps that will happen for other reasons. But it will leave school refusal largely untouched, unless we are to lock them up in ever greater numbers. Decriminalizing the language and seeing children who do not attend school as 'children in need', rather than morally deviant, is the approach advocated by the Children Act, still less than three years old. It is difficult to see why such an approach should be abandoned before it has even been tried.

Making welfare work
There has been general agreement that Part III of the Act about the provision of services to help families manage their children is the part which has yet to be implemented in terms of proper resources. Society has not yet established that welfare doesn't work. We know that other approaches don't, but we have yet to build a society in

which parents who are struggling to manage their responsibilities can turn to the local authority for help, without fear of condemnation, with practical alternatives on offer to help them do a better job.

We don't have enough foster-carers and family aides to work alongside parents in managing children with behavioural and emotional difficulties. We don't have the special educational support services at the level we need so that such children can receive appropriate education in mainstream schools rather than causing havoc or drifting away. We don't have enough family centres where whole families can go for therapeutic counselling and help. We don't have the jobs through which people, whose self-esteem has been battered by poverty and unemployment, can begin to believe that it's worth bothering with what's happening to their children. We don't have sufficient advice and counselling services to stop relationships disintegrating under pressure so that children won't grow up feeling angry, unwanted or confused.

All we can do is seek to enable children and their parents to act responsibly and persuade them that their own best interests are served by regular school attendance. The idea that such behaviour has to be imposed by force betrays the fact that it does not bring, of itself, sufficient reward. If school is so wonderful, why do so many reject it? Will children only go under threat? I am convinced that the only viable way forward is to work towards an education system designed to meet the needs of *every* child. In short, to make it so good that everyone will want to go. Which brings us to the second tension.

Uniformity v. diversity

The government has made much of its intention to create an education system with more choice and diversity. This is said to be the aim of all the recent legislation: to improve the opportunity for choice by parents and enable a wider variety of good quality educational provision. In practice, however, the diversity appears to be within a very limited range and the choice seems to rest more with schools than with parents, especially those parents whose children feel least motivated to attend.

We will see increasing specialism within schools in the coming years: schools concentrating on music, sport, the arts or technology; schools with entrance examinations and various forms of selection for at least some of their intake; schools run without the involvement of the LEA but managed by the Funding Agency; small schools in rural areas saved from closure by groups of parents who have obtained sufficient money to rescue the building and reopen it as a new grant maintained school; religious schools supporting a variety of denominational and cultural traditions. Which, if any, of these will address the needs of those for whom no kind of school has much value at present?

The limits to choice
Diversity means little for the child on the urban housing estate where there is only one school and the opportunity of travelling to others is not available, even assuming they would be welcome there. LEAs cannot be expected to fund the cost of travel to any school of the parents' choice, wherever it is, so this means that only those who can afford it can select from a wider geographical area. Such a requirement would render the efficient use of resources impossible and would lead to children being ferried all over the place, undermining parental involvement even further.

For large numbers of children, especially those whose parents have little or no freedom about where they live (a power so often assumed by the free-marketeers), there is no choice and no diversity either, unless the child ends up excluded when all that is then on offer may be minimal home tuition in the face of refusal from all other available schools to let them in.

Nearly all secondary schools are (a) large, a factor in itself which means that a percentage of children feel uncomfortable in such an environment; (b) required to teach the National Curriculum with only very limited scope for experimentation to meet individual needs; and (c) expected to concentrate on the achievement of academic success as measured by national league tables of examination performance. The Dearing review should mean some significant changes and perhaps National Vocational Qualifications will one day be seen as equal in status with strings of A levels, though past experience suggests that this is unlikely.

What we need is a clear recognition that raising educational standards is not the same as trying to force all children into a mould designed primarily for the children of the professional classes. So many concepts which are taken for granted as signs of a 'good' school: academic standards, discipline, order, uniform, homework, good exam results, high rates of staying on post-16, effective PTAs, etc., are value-judgements based on a particular perception of what a school 'ought' to be.

There is simply not the consensus about this in society that some legislators believe. Why do so many parents stay away and take so little interest in what goes on at school? Why do they not make more use of all the opportunities given to them by recent legislation?

Because they know that school hasn't changed all that much since they were there. They were made to feel like failures then and they feel pretty much the same now. They know their child will bring the school little credit; they are intimidated by the size of the place; they don't know the teachers personally; they feel as uncomfortable in their presence as they used to feel as children. It's not *their* school; it's just the school. And there are more pressing things to deal with like jobs and bills and managing till Friday.

I appreciate that this sounds like caricature. It is not intended to be at all patronizing. I can only say that vast numbers of individuals come into my mind as I write; ordinary, decent, caring, hardworking parents and their children, who simply felt totally out of place at school and had no choice at all over what went on there. It is remarkable how many of them make sure their children go so often. But to expect more is simply unrealistic, until we can be sure that every child has access to provision which is right for them and that they and their parents have played an active part in choosing it.

Alternatives to school

The best hope for such ideas is a *real* range of educational facilities: small schools, alternative schools, off-site and specialist units, imaginative schemes such as the 'Bridge courses' pioneered by Cities in Schools or the School Leavers Project in Islington – places where children can be educated but which don't feel like school. This is potentially rather dangerous as it may tend to label certain children as failures and lead to perceptions of such places as 'sinks' or 'sin-bins'. If anything, there are now less options than there used to be; as resources have increasingly been concentrated in the hands of schools, many such units have closed.

The Education Act 1993 standardizes the idea of 'portability' – the money following a permanently excluded child into subsequent provision, but usually it is not enough to fund alternatives which tend to be more expensive if they are on a smaller scale. If there is a real commitment to diversity, this flexibility should be available for *all* pupils who need it, not just those who have got as far as exclusion. What matters most is that the school or unit meets the child's needs, not where it figures on some arbitrary league table of academic achievement. For all the talk, only GCSEs and staying-on rates really seem to count in the government's mind. (The inclusion of special schools for children with severe learning difficulties in the performance tables was perhaps the most ridiculous example of this obsession.)

An open market

Children are now counted in terms of their cash value; they are 'worth' £1,800 or more a year during their final years of compulsory education. One way of moving in the right direction would be to recognize this by some kind of 'voucher' system through which all parents could purchase a package of educational provision from a variety of sources, ie, not simply as a means for a few parents to gain access to scarce educational opportunity which would still be dependent on selection.

Parents do not have to educate their children at a school, but there is no way they can access that money if they choose the 'otherwise' option or if they wish to use alternative provision. Surely there is far greater scope for enabling them to buy in to all kinds of educational experience and many would do better to take advantage of opportunities outside traditional schools? All parents (except perhaps those above a certain income) could be given an equal age-weighted package of resources with which to purchase education for their children, with extra for those with special educational needs. As envisaged by supporters of voucher schemes in the past, they would be free to use it in the private sector (which might also mean the end of any LEA schemes for assisting with the cost of places) as well as in local schools or elsewhere.

Why should such opportunities exist only for the most able or most motivated pupils? Why should people not be able to spend their voucher at a smaller unit specializing in children who have lost interest in school? Or in employing a private tutor, buying correspondence courses, tapping into work experience and training schemes or any mixture of all these? Why should conventional schools have the market to themselves? Under such a system they would have to compete with other providers offering specialist provision where it is demanded – surely an approach quite compatible with current political thinking and offering real choice and diversity to those who need it most?

'Pupil referral units' might offer hope to some such families in the short-term, though they will fail if they are not properly resourced, are full after the first week or develop a poor reputation. Children will not go if the units are perceived as poor quality or as a punishment. Greater use of local FE colleges is becoming a real possibility now that the Further and Higher Education Act 1992 has given them the freedom to recruit students under the minimum school-leaving age – another excellent opportunity for parents to make use of a voucher system (see also p.123 below).

Of course it would have to be monitored and the various facilities inspected in some way, but by LEAs more concerned to enable than to enforce. This whole debate is about rigidity versus flexibility. Real choice, real diversity means that parents should be offered a range of possibilities rather than being prosecuted for failing to take advantage of the only one on offer. At present, not going may be the only choice the child can make; all the rest is taken for granted. The more options there are, the more likely we are to make that match in a way which motivates and encourages them. Simply telling them what to do, in ever louder voices, will take us nowhere.

Dependence v. independence

This tension is more subtle but every bit as important. It is time society made up its mind about teenagers. Are they children, subject to parental authority, not yet ready to make their own way in the world, in need of control by others; or are they ready to be listened to, able to take control of their own lives, capable of making at least some decisions for themselves and taking responsibility for what happens to them? Nearly all our problems with truancy and school refusal come in the last two years of compulsory education: a time in a teenager's life when no one, least of all the teenagers themselves, knows how to define their status.

We send mixed messages and have conflicting expectations. The history of educational provision has shown an ever-lengthening period during which children are kept in a dependent relationship with their parents. School-leaving age may well be raised a little later in the future, or all 16- and 17-year olds may be required to stay on into some form of further education. You have no democratic say at this age and even the Children Act calls all those under 18 'children'. The DfE's circular on sex education, published in 1994, gave parents the right to withdraw their child, including even those in the sixth form, with no requirement to consult them and obtain their views anywhere in the process.

Children have few rights in education; they may, for example, be given no opportunity to be heard in their own exclusion procedure. There is no charter for children, only their parents. We are still talking about them as if they were not here, as we used to do with people with disabilities until we discovered how offensive it is. As job opportunities have declined and benefits for those under 18 have been virtually withdrawn, the period of financial dependence grows ever longer, for some young adults even way beyond their 18th birthday. Housing policy, reductions in student grants and the punitive attitude towards 'young ladies who get pregnant just to jump the housing queue' have made it all but impossible for youngsters to move into independent accommodation without massive parental backing. In some senses childhood goes on for ever.

The 'mature minor'

Yet at 16, several months before many Year 11 pupils can leave school, young people may legally be sexually active (provided they are heterosexual or lesbian). They can, in practice, move in with a partner even without their parents' consent as no court would be likely to consider making orders to resolve such disputes, and any orders made in the past about where they should live will normally end at 16. Even before 16, ever since the ruling in the 'Gillick' case in 1985, it has been accepted that parents' rights to make decisions about their children gradually have to give way to the rights of children 'of sufficient intelligence and understanding' to make decisions for themselves.

Physically, young people mature more quickly than ever; menstruation starts earlier and estimates suggest that significant numbers of 15-year-olds and younger are already sexually experienced, many of them, especially girls, forming committed relationships with older young adults. Despite the law about consent, no prosecution will now follow in such a situation unless exploitation or abuse are involved. Notwithstanding new restrictions on what teachers may say to them, many teenagers want to know about AIDS or contraception in order to protect themselves, not just as questions of academic or moral debate. Some of them need to know it as a matter of considerable urgency. Advice and prescriptions will be given to under-16s in clinics, etc. without parental consent if appropriate.

Many pupils live lifestyles outside school hours which reflect a culture previously available only to adults. The media and advertisers increasingly target teenagers; they have status and choice and many have enough money of their own through parents or part-time employment (legal from age 13 onwards) to be significant consumers. Many carry domestic or caring responsibilities either for younger children or parents. The UN Convention on the Rights of the Child, ratified by the UK in 1991, demands they be recognized as individuals in their own right, with their own legitimate opinions which should at least be heard and taken seriously.

Schools in the firing line

This tension between dependence and independence is often at its sharpest at school, not least because of the different approaches to children and young people by different government departments. The Department for Education has never really accepted the Children Act because it conflicts with its view of schools as socializing agents which should be reinforcing (appropriate) parental values. Parents are the consumers of education, not children, so their needs dominate. At the same time, under the guidance of the Department of Health, school nurses, social workers and others have been giving their 'service users', including older children, every opportunity to express themselves independently in line with the Act's general approach. There is a fundamental conflict at the heart of our child care system.

At school they are children; for the rest of their lives they are adults in the making who happen to be young. And many cannot handle the confusion. They find the petty rules and regulations at school irksome and insulting to their intelligence; they are looking for more equal relationships with adults such as they are used to outside. The dress codes may seem very generous and reasonable to us but to them they are a symbol of their status as a child, to be resisted and stretched to their limits wherever possible. Adults in authority have to earn their respect; they will not get it simply for their status.

I know all this strikes many people of my generation and older as disgraceful; but we have created these monsters! Society has placed its schools in an impossible position. It is asking them to keep children as children longer than ever; let them learn to behave, do as they are told, have no say in their own right, while we have created a wider culture in which there is every possible pressure on them to mature as quickly as possible. Outside school, it has suited us to have children reach maturity quicker; they have had to learn to cope with our failed relationships and the fact that adults aren't perfect. We no longer believe that we must pretend or make sacrifices 'for the sake of the children'; let them sort it out for themselves – it will do them good.

We have to listen to the 15-year old who says she can't stand going to school because it's full of kids! There is a serious point behind her discomfort. She is desperate to grow up. Every other influence on her life is telling her that she is there already, in control, responsible. The teacher is telling her to take her make-up off and go home for a proper pair of shoes! I know it sounds trivial but it really is incidents like that which stop children going to school for weeks at a time. They see only endless months of school stretching into the distance, long after they feel out of place and bored with the whole experience. Life outside has moved on: life at school has stood still.

A new approach?
Our difficulties with older children are in part because society has become out of step with itself. For example, when regulations were introduced in 1933 to restrict the employment of children, the minimum age at which a young person could work was fixed at 13 – one year before the age when they could leave school altogether. It is still 13, but now we have three years of limbo to get through: old enough to work, but not old enough to leave school and get a job. Things which children can legally do for work experience are not open to them for proper employment. I seriously wonder whether it is time to call their bluff and let them move into the adult world at an earlier age if that is what they want.

Maybe school as we have traditionally known it should end at age 14 again and from then on all young people would move on into some form of further education, training or employment. GCSEs, A levels etc would become an integrated process for those who remain at school, but some would be able to escape if they feel they have had enough. Such an approach would then undermine the argument that there is no point in bothering because there's nothing to look forward to – a particular problem for children who have already lost all realistic hope of GCSEs by the end of Year 9 and who, in all honesty, have little reason left for coming.

Many if not most young people will choose more school because they are still happy to fit in with its expectations and they are planning a career involving lengthy study. Some will choose college, specialist units or perhaps new kinds of high schools where you don't have to go all day every day and you can wear what you like. Some will be ready to do a proper day's work and all they ever really wanted to do was to join dad on the farm or serve in the shop where they've been working on Saturdays. Some will want to mix work and training in new forms of apprenticeships with real qualifications at the end. (In effect, this would be a re-invention of 'continuation studies'.) Some will pick up further training opportunities later when they are a bit older and wiser or have a clearer idea of what they want to do. None of these routes should close down the others.

If they're not willing to do any of these then let them do some kind of service to the community in return for an allowance in their own right which they don't get otherwise. As long as there were real guarantees that *no one* would be left totally destitute or homeless I would be happy to see some kind of carrot and stick to encourage the reluctant. But I suspect there wouldn't be all that many as long as there were sufficient alternatives available to reflect the full range of needs.

Sharing the responsibility
Truancy as we know it would, in my opinion, all but disappear, though we would still have to face all the other reasons why children might not attend school regularly even at a much earlier age. There will always be families with problems. Parents would still have a duty to make it all happen up to age 14, though after that young people should be able to make more decisions for themselves and be expected to take at least some of the responsibility if they make mistakes. Perhaps the EWO's/ESW's job should be to make sure that no one is overlooked and working environments in particular would need careful regulation and monitoring.

Is all this a step backwards or forwards? Reformers thought they were doing the right thing by removing teenagers from the world of employment; I would be happy to see some of them go back again, properly supervised, paid and trained, though there would have to be a determined attempt to create the jobs for them to go to. Calling for more freedom of choice is usually a right-wing agenda. Yet championing the rights of children to be given more say over their own lives is usually a cause of the left. Maybe that suggests that the balance is about right.

CONCLUSIONS

Through teenagers' eyes

I am not saying that we should just drop our young people in at the deep end of the adult world and leave them to it. This is not just an argument for withdrawing the 'nanny' state and letting the weakest go to the wall. Safety-nets for children can never be too wide. No matter how much they may do to frustrate our attempts to help them, we must never write them off as beyond hope. Children do need to accept that they cannot always have things exactly how they want them. But we adults – parents, professionals and politicians – may actually be making things much more difficult for our teenagers than they need be.

They and their families will continue to need help, advice and support; but such services should be primarily about ensuring entitlement and empowering parents and children to take responsible control of their lives. Some are profoundly damaged by everything that has happened to them in the past. We are only just beginning to ask as a nation whether the consequences of broken relationships, disrupted family life, poverty and unemployment may be far more significant than we have liked to think. It is inevitable that some children will choose school as the way of demonstrating their general unhappiness with life, either within their own families or within the wider society, because at present their experience there is so often seen as restricting, not liberating.

I have nothing but anecdotal evidence to offer, but it is clear from my caseload that children can be very angry with their parents, and with all of us, when they are left to cope with the consequences of our past failures. They often do not see why they should be expected to carry on as if nothing has happened and behave themselves as adults wish. They feel vulnerable, betrayed and alone. Teachers may be a particular focus for their hostility. They love their parents, despite everything. Teachers, EWOs/ESWs and the rest represent 'them' – authority without the feelings.

Nothing to lose?

Thankfully, most children grow out of truancy; with them it is more of an irritant than a major social issue. I really don't believe we should get too het up about it. It is an inevitable part of a compulsory system. It has always been there and it always will be; in many ways it is a perfectly healthy sign. We need young people to be able to think for themselves. Some of what they say about the inappropriateness and poor quality of their education is correct. But on the whole teachers, parents and children try very hard to get it right and they are successful for most of the time. There is much that can be done. Efficient, caring vigilance is dealing with most of the problems. We do not need more laws or more powers to deal with these pupils; only more encouragement, resources, time, vision and imagination.

There is a far more worrying group of children, much smaller, probably no more than 1 or 2 per cent of the school population overall, though larger in our cities, who simply feel that the whole business is nothing to do with them. They have never experienced education, only schools. They, and often their parents too, feel no stake in the nation; no sense of purpose in either their personal or community lives. Their 'truancy' is incidental; a symptom of the problem, not the problem itself. They are the lost souls of the system; some of them literally being abandoned to their fate by a society that has no place for them. Some children effectively 'disappear', unknown to any agency; the descendants of the 'beggards and trampers' of the last century; a counter-culture at odds with the rest of us.

However we structure the provision, the essential debate is about whether we believe that education and training for employment are part of society's care for *all* its younger citizens or some kind of obstacle course through which all must go even though only some achieve anything. The key questions which most disaffected young people are asking us are, 'What does it offer *me*? What exactly is it all for? What have I got to lose by not going?' Do we not still have a model of education which is essentially based on the public schools, designed to allow the best to rise to the top and to make sure the rest conform sufficiently to avoid rocking the boat? Does the curriculum have any real relevance for the majority of children's lives?

Many teenagers have seen through the system, as they have seen through the supposed security of the family and the merits of thrift. Why should they postpone gratification when adult society is built on getting what you want as quickly as possible? They know that they are on their own. For far too many this leads, at a depressingly early age, to the conclusion that there is not much point in bothering. The only game in which they are invited to play is one which they know they will lose. Indeed some feel that they have lost before they even start.

Hope for the future?

A future education system should be one in which even such individuals feel so much at home that they do not need people like me knocking on the door trying to convince them that they should go. 'School' will be one of the key places in their lives where they are made to feel good about themselves, even if things are pretty desperate elsewhere. They will find there a sense of a personal place in a community which recognizes them as having a valuable contribution to play.

They will have opportunity to exercise influence in positive, not merely negative ways. Their needs will be addressed and their self-esteem enhanced. When they make mistakes, which of course they will, or if they need help, there will be people and services there to work things through with them, not in a punitive way but in ways which take them seriously and move them on to something new. They will be given space to grow; to become themselves, not to be moulded to external expectations of who they 'ought' to be.

Perhaps such a hope is unrealistic, but we have lost the battle once we become cynical and disillusioned. As the motto of the National Association of Social Workers in Education says: 'For every child a chance'. We would certainly need different kinds of schools. Such a society could never be brought about by teachers alone and it is unreasonable to expect them to do so. But as one who is asked to help control some of society's less enthusiastic participants, I cannot see a future in any other direction, not at any rate a future which carries any attraction.

More and more blaming will only make things worse. Of course parents shouldn't walk away from their responsibilities, but there's no point in just condemning them when they do. Of course they should work at solving their problems and keep their children under control, but some start from such a disadvantaged and hopeless position, and have access to so little help, that no amount of nagging will change them. Of course children should behave themselves and take every advantage from their education, but if they don't, more creative solutions are needed than those which are currently available. Parents and children need understanding, not rejection, which seems to be all that many feel at present.

Truancy, school refusal, condoned absence, unauthorized absence – call it what you will; at their most extreme they are all pointing the way to much bigger issues. The truth about at least some truancy is that it tells us something is wrong, not just with those who do it but with the community we adults have built for our children to live in. The system fails half of those who go through it. If there is a real concern to build something better which is more appropriate to the 21st century, maybe it's time to listen to those whose needs have often been overlooked in the last 150 years – the losers: still picking up the pieces, still the last to be heard in our agonizing over how to do things better.

Index